GREAT HEROES
of MYTHOLOGY

GREAT HEROES
of MYTHOLOGY

PETRA PRESS

MetroBooks

An Imprint of Friedman/Fairfax Publishers

© 1997 by Michael Friedman Publishing Group, Inc.

All rights reserved. No part of this publication may be reproduced, stored in a retrieval system, or transmitted, in any form or by any means, electronic, mechanical, photocopying, recording, or otherwise, without prior written permission from the publisher.

Library of Congress Cataloging-in-Publication Data

Press, Petra.
    Great heroes of mythology / Petra Press.
       p.   cm.
    Includes bibliographical references and index.
    ISBN 1-56799-433-4
    1. Heroes—Mythology. I. TItle.
BL325.H46P74   1997
398.22—dc21   97-9045

Editor: Tony Burgess
Designers: Garrett Schuh, Diego Vainesman
Photography Editor: Deidra Gorgos
Production Manager: Camille Lee

Color separations by Bright Arts Graphics (S) Pte Ltd
Printed in England by Butler and Tanner Limited

For bulk purchases and special sales, please contact:
Friedman/Fairfax Publishers
Attention: Sales Department
15 West 26th Street
New York, NY 10010
212/685-6610 FAX 212/685-1307

Visit our website:
http://www.metrobooks.com

CONTENTS

Introduction
What Makes a Hero?
6

Chapter One
Heroes of Egyptian and Middle Eastern Mythology
10

Chapter Two
Heroes of Classical Greek Mythology
28

Chapter Three
Heroes of the British Isles
44

Chapter Four
Heroes of Scandinavian Mythology
66

Chapter Five
Heroes of Asian Mythology
84

Chapter Six
Heroes of Oceanic and Australian Mythology
102

Chapter Seven
Heroes of African Mythology
118

Chapter Eight
Heroes of Central and South American Mythology
134

Chapter Nine
Heroes of Native North American Mythology
152

Conclusion 170
Bibliography 172   Index 173

Introduction
What Makes a Hero?

Myths, Legends, and Folktales

The word *myth* comes from the Greek word *mythos*, which originally meant "word" or "story." Later, in about the fourth century B.C., the Greeks added another word for story, *logos*, meaning "word of truth." After that, *logos* was used to refer to "true" stories, historical accounts written by recognizable authors, and *mythos* came to mean the anonymous stories that were handed down (and embellished) by storytellers over the centuries until someone finally wrote them down. In other words, *mythos* came to mean fiction.

A legend is also an anonymous story handed down and embellished by storytellers over the centuries until someone finally writes it down. The difference between a myth and a legend, however, is that a legend is based on an actual historical figure or event.

A folktale, too, is an anonymous story handed down over time, but the difference between folktale and myth is that a folktale usually conveys a social message (that youngsters should respect their elders, for example) rather than dealing with the more cosmic subjects of death, heroism, tragic love, or the meaning of the universe. Folktales are also usually the product of societies which are based on agriculture.

A Search for Meaning

Whether myths are believed as truth or merely enjoyed as entertaining stories, they have had an almost magical appeal to every generation since humans invented language. While every culture has its own unique mythology, scientists and philosophers as early as the seventeenth century became fascinated with the similar themes and characters that seemed to surface all over the world. They began collecting and comparing myths and came up with some interesting theories.

At first, many Europeans held that myths were nothing more than strangely distorted Bible stories, while others were soon arguing that they were primitive, symbolic efforts to explain natural phenomena. One British anthropologist, James Frazer, proposed that myths show us how the welfare of each society depends on how well its kings rule.

In the twentieth century, scientists, philosophers, and anthropologists began looking into the human mind and psyche for answers. The Austrian psychoanalyst Sigmund Freud proposed that myths give shape to peoples' frightening unconscious fears and urges and provide a nonthreatening way to deal with them. For example, Freud claimed that the Greek myth of Oedipus, who killed his father and married his mother, symbolizes a stage all young boys go through when they feel hostility toward their fathers and attraction to their mothers.

The Swiss psychoanalyst Carl Jung took that theory a bit further and suggested that the reason myths have such a powerful hold on human imaginations is that they contain the same "archetypes" or principal symbolic characters in every human psyche or unconscious. By reflecting these universal archetypes, myths not only help people work out individual conflicts, but help them relate to society. These archetypes are characters like the Wise Old Man, the Good Mother, and the Fool.

opposite
One of the Twelve Labors of the Greek hero Heracles was to slay the Hydra, a nine-headed serpent which lived in a swamp near the city of Lerna. Whenever Heracles cut off one head, two more grew in its place.

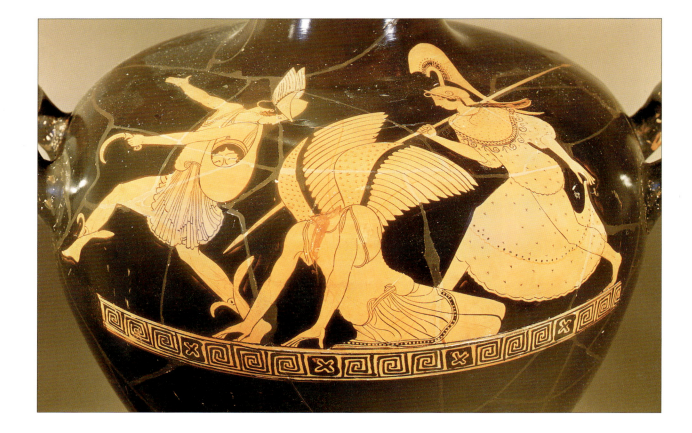

This red-figure Greek amphora from about 330 B.C. shows the hero Perseus wearing the winged sandals and cap of darkness that enabled him to behead the snake-haired gorgon Medusa.

Traditional Heroes

One of the most powerful mythological archetypes is that of the Hero. The myths and legends of every culture feature extraordinary individuals who perform superhuman feats to aid society. Usually (although not always) these individuals are humans with supernatural strength and/or other magical abilities. Sometimes, however, the heroes are half mortal and half god, such as the Greek hero Heracles, whose father was the god Zeus but whose mother was mortal. Sometimes heroes are not human at all but gods who defy other immortals to aid humankind, such as Prometheus, who stole fire from heaven for the benefit of mortals only to be savagely punished by Zeus for his crime.

Cultural heroes can play a number of different roles. There are traditional warrior heroes like Gilgamesh and Beowulf, hero-kings such as Theseus and Arthur, tragic heroic lovers such as Sigmund and Brynhild, even unlikely and often reluctant commoner heroes such as Aladdin.

Traditional hero types usually have a number of things in common: a call to adventure; a long, dangerous voyage and/or search for some person, place, or thing; the overcoming of formidable trials; the slaying of grotesque monsters or deadly enemies; and the rescue of the poor and helpless. They all either have superhuman powers themselves or they get help from the gods.

Not all the traits of traditional heroes are necessarily admirable, however. It depends on the culture. In ancient Greece, for example, heroes were worshipped for their superhuman strength, athletic ability, skill with weapons, and actions that benefited their community. There was no further expectation of morality. For example, the Greek term hero could be used to describe a homicidal boxer like Cleomedes of Astypalia. When the man was disqualified for accidentally killing his opponent in the Olympic games, he became so angry that he knocked down a schoolhouse on top of sixty children. Yet he was still considered a hero.

Heracles is considered by many to be the Greek hero of all time, yet he was portrayed as a glutton, womanizer, rapist, and drunk, known as much for his brutal outbursts of rage as for his feats of superhuman strength.

Trickster Heroes

Many cultures throughout the world, especially those of North and South America, Oceania, and Africa, also feature another type of hero altogether—the trickster. The trickster is a rebel against authority and the breaker of all taboos. He is a creator and culture-bringer who is at the same time an imp and mischief-maker. He represents the lowly, small, and poor by playing pranks on the proud, big, and rich. Often the trickster hero is a shape-shifter who can assume the features of a man one minute and look like a coyote, bird, or rabbit the next.

Native American trickster figures such as Old Man Coyote, Raven, and Hare also play the role of cosmic joker, delighting their audiences when they outwit the enemies of humankind, even though they often make some ridiculous and even disastrous mistakes in the process. African cultures have similar shape-shifting animal tricksters such as the hare, tortoise, and spider that use their intelligence to outwit and frustrate the rich and powerful.

But like the more traditional heroes, tricksters definitely have their faults. They are often portrayed as selfish, lazy, vain, and envious, and almost always have amazingly gluttonous appetites.

Heroic Literature

Every culture on earth has developed its own rich collection of myths and has celebrated the exploits of mythological heroes in heroic literature such as the Greek *Iliad*, Mesopotamia's *Epic of Gilgamesh*, Mexico's *Popl Vuh*, the Anglo-Saxon *Beowulf*, the Native American Spider Woman tales, and Persia's *Arabian Nights*, to name just a very few.

It would be impossible to touch on all the heroes of every culture in a single book, but we have included several of the most vivid and memorable stories from each major culture in this volume. Consider this book a starting point, a place to whet your appetite for the incredible feast of heroic literature that awaits you.

Nigerian sculptors have used human and animal myths as inspirations for highly stylized bronze, terra cotta, and wood sculptures since the fourth century B.C. Sculptures such as this one are meant to tell an entire story drawn from the rich mythology of western Africa.

Chapter 1

Heroes of Egyptian and Middle Eastern Mythology

The myths of ancient Egypt were stories passed down by the priests and kings who tended the complex religious cults by which the many gods were cared for, and they were only concerned with the relationships between the different gods, never with individual humans. Although Egyptians covered their temples with many images of their gods' struggles, relatively few of their myths were ever written down. Most have had to be reconstructed from indirect sources such as funerary texts, cult rituals and hymns, and texts of magic.

Unlike Ancient Egypt, the Middle Eastern cultures that developed in the fertile valley of the Tigris and Euphrates rivers recorded their myths at length. Although the official state religion, tended to by important priests, involved a large pantheon of gods, the common people of Sumeria practiced an animistic faith that held that the world was populated by demons such as the "scorpion-man." A large number of texts were written to recount the legends and myths of semi-divine folk heroes such as Gilgamesh.

1

Isis and Osiris
A myth from ancient Egypt

This myth tells of a mighty pharaoh named Osiris, who, thousands of years ago, ruled the ancient land of Egypt along the river Nile. Tall and slender, he was a handsome man with beautifully plaited hair and a royal crown made of ivory and precious stones. It is said he was the great-grandson of Ra, the great god who created the world, and he ruled Egypt wisely and righteously for many years.

Over time Osiris taught his beloved subjects to give up their evil and savage ways and become civilized. He outlawed cannibalism and gave them a code of laws to live by that brought peace and order to what had been a chaotic and often frightening place to live. He showed people how to cultivate the rich earth of the Nile Valley to grow food, and taught them how to make bread and wine.

Osiris took as his wife his twin sister Isis, whom he had loved and embraced while they were still in their mother's womb. Isis was tall and slender like her brother, with beautiful green eyes and regal elegance. Her royal attire included a tall helmet with a gold disk set between two horns. Isis, too, took an active part in ruling the country and educating her people. She was also the mother of a young son named Horus.

Unfortunately, Osiris and Isis had a younger brother named Set who was the opposite of Osiris in every way. He was short and repulsively ugly with scraggly red hair, a pointed nose, and very bad teeth. He secretly hated Osiris and desperately wanted to be king of Egypt himself so he could reinstate some of the old practices Osiris had outlawed, such as cannibalism.

There came a day when Osiris announced to his wife that it was time he left Egypt and set out to bring the blessings of civilization to the rest of the world. He knew he was leaving Egypt in capable hands, for Isis was as great a ruler as he himself. So it was settled, and Osiris left for Asia the next day. He took no soldiers and no weapons with him, for he believed he could win the people over with music, kind words, and reason.

Set would have loved to take advantage of Osiris' absence to take over the kingdom, but Isis was in complete control and made it quite impossible. So Set hatched an evil plot for the day of his brother's return from Asia. He enlisted the aid of seventy-two accomplices to hold a banquet in honor of Osiris's return.

The feast went as planned. After a delicious dinner, Set announced that it was time for some entertainment, in the form of a contest. He

opposite
This gold and lapis figure from Egypt's Thirteenth Dynasty (c.850 B.C.) shows the mummified Egyptian King Osiris flanked by his son Horus and widow and sister Isis. Osiris was murdered and dismembered by his evil brother Set.

Heroes of Egyptian and Middle Eastern Mythology 13

In this detail from the sarcophagus of Butehamon, a pharaoh of Egypt's Twenty-first Dynasty, Isis and her sister Nephthys guard the throne of King Osiris. According to legend, they watched over his mummified body in the form of sparrow hawks.

ordered his servants to bring in a beautiful gold and silver chest studded with jewels. The chest was to be both the challenge and the prize. It was simple; whoever could fit into the chest could claim it.

Now it happened that the seventy-two people Set chose to attend the banquet were all a little overweight and therefore too large to fit into the narrow chest. Since Set had had the chest built to his brother's exact measurements, he knew Osiris would fit into the chest perfectly. To humor his brother after everyone else had failed, Osiris climbed into the chest. Instantly, all seventy-two of the guests leaped on the chest, slammed down the lid, and nailed it shut. Then they threw the chest into the river Nile.

The river carried Osiris's coffin out into the open sea where it floated until it finally washed ashore on the Phoenician coast near a tamarisk tree. The tree reached out with its branches, grabbed the chest, and pulled it into its trunk where it remained hidden for many years. One day a local king came across the tree and cut it down to use as a pillar in his palace. But a remarkable thing happened: the pillar started to give off a marvelous odor of honey and fresh summer blossoms that could be smelled all the way to Egypt.

One day Isis caught wind of the wondrous smell. She had been in deep mourning ever since Set had announced that Osiris was dead and had abandoned all of her royal duties to search for her husband's body. While she was busy searching from one end of Egypt to the other, Set seized the throne. He brought back the savage ways of old, practiced cannibalism, and ruled tyrannically.

Isis knew that the tree in Phoenicia that gave off the incredible smell must contain the body of Osiris and left immediately to bring it back. She carried it back to Egypt where she hid it on a small island in the middle of the Nile until she could arrange for a proper funeral. By unfortunate chance, however, Set came upon the chest one day when he was out hunting. When he recognized it, he pried open the lid, drew his sword, and cut the body of Osiris into fourteen pieces, which he then scattered all over Egypt.

It took Isis more than two years to find all the pieces of her husband, and even then she only managed to retrieve thirteen of them, for one piece had been eaten by crabs. Isis joined the pieces together, and when she was finished, Osiris woke up as if from a deep sleep. Having been smothered, drowned, trapped in a tree trunk, hacked into fourteen pieces, and then embalmed, Osiris was weary and chose to ascend the ladder to the crystal floor of heaven. He left it to his son, Horus, to avenge his death and save Egypt.

Horus did just that. He and Set fought many battles, until finally one day Horus took a sharp harpoon and plunged it into Set's brain. Horus took over the throne and from then on ruled Egypt as wisely and kindly as his parents had done before him.

Gilgamesh the Wrestler
A Sumerian Tale from Mesopotamia

It is said that King Gilgamesh was two-thirds god and one-third human. He was born in the royal palace at Uruk, the son of a god-king and a mother who "knew all knowledge." He grew up to be a strong, powerful, and courageous king who became known as a great hunter of lions and wild bulls, a superb wrestler of awesome strength, and a heroic soldier.

His people worshiped the two-thirds of Gilgamesh that were a god, but were not always happy with the one-third of him that was a man. Gilgamesh was a handsome man with an unquenchable desire for women, and he saw nothing wrong with snatching maidens from their fathers' homes or wives who were out shopping in the marketplace, throwing them over his shoulder, and riding off with them. When he was not on the battlefield or out hunting, he strode about town with a pet monkey on each shoulder looking for more women to kidnap, his black

This bronze figure from the ninth or tenth century B.C. represents Osiris, who, after his death, was enthroned as judge of the underworld. Egyptians believed that when they died, Osiris weighed their souls to determine if their spirits were pure enough to join the gods in the underworld.

Heroes of Egyptian and Middle Eastern Mythology 15

beard thick and curly and his long, wavy black hair falling below his shoulders.

This practice caused much anger and resentment among his people, but there was no one in the city or the surrounding countryside who dared to challenge the king in battle or defy him in open combat. So Gilgamesh continued to swagger through the streets, stealing maidens and bragging about his hunting exploits.

Finally, in desperation, a council of city elders visited the temple of Aruru, the great mother goddess, and pleaded with her to create a man strong and powerful enough to defeat Gilgamesh. Taking pity on the distraught people of Uruk, Aruru reached down from her throne to the riverbank, scooped up some clay, shaped it into an image, and then blew life into it. And that was how Enkidu was born.

Enkidu had the hoofs, thighs, and tail of a bull, yet from the waist up was an incredibly muscular man. He could run as fast as a gazelle and often used his strength and speed to come to the aid of his wild animal friends when they were being chased by hunters. In time, Enkidu's daring and swiftness became a legend around Uruk and Gilgamesh became annoyed and jealous.

Thinking that taming the creature was the only way to diminish its power, Gilgamesh came up with a plan. He promised a beautiful courtesan gold and jewels if she waited at sunset near Enkidu's watering hole and seduced him. When his animal friends saw the woman, they fled in fear but Enkidu was too entranced with the woman's beauty to run. She used soft words and flattery to make him fall in love with her, then whispered to him about the delights and comforts of city life until she convinced him to return with her to Uruk.

When they arrived at Gilgamesh's palace, the astonished and awed Enkidu allowed the palace women to bathe him, trim his hair and beard, and even get him to put on a shirt. Over the next few weeks, they taught him table manners and how to behave at the royal court. As Enkidu became more and more civilized, he lost some of his brute strength; at the same time, he sharpened his intelligence and developed a strong sense of right and wrong.

One night, a drunk Gilgamesh left a party with a group of young men, including Enkidu, to roam the streets of Uruk in search of female companionship. However, when Gilgamesh was about to lead the group into a particularly evil house of debauchery, Enkidu was so outraged that he barred the door and refused to let Gilgamesh pass. Shaking with anger, Gilgamesh threw a powerful blow at his jaw that would have flattened a normal person, but Enkidu neatly parried the blow and grabbed Gilgamesh by the shoulders. Soon the two were wrestling and rolling on the ground.

It was the first time in his life that Gilgamesh had wrestled with someone of equal strength. For hours a gathering crowd watched as they grappled with each other, sweat pouring from their mighty muscles, but neither could budge the other. Then, suddenly, Gilgamesh released his hold on Enkidu and burst out laughing. Soon Enkidu was laughing too. All their anger had vanished and they realized that out of their struggle a friendship had been born that would last for the rest of their lives.

From that moment on, Gilgamesh and Enkidu were inseparable. Enkidu even sat at King Gilgamesh's side when he held court. The people of Uruk were delighted at this new friendship, because Enkidu had an amazing influence on his new friend. From then on, Gilgamesh gave up the evil habits that had caused them so much concern. In spite of the peace, prosperity, and luxury of life in Uruk, however (or perhaps because of it), the two became increasingly restless and before long they set off on a series of remarkable adventures.

There are many stories that tell their exploits: how they subdued the hideous Huwawa, the giant guardian of the cedar forest, how they almost brought down the curse of the gods when Gilgamesh made the mistake of spurning the advances of Ishtar, the goddess of love, and how they slew the formidable Bull of Heaven.

After many such adventures that brought the two heroes much fame, Enkidu was felled by a fatal illness. Grief-stricken and realizing for the first time that he too would have to die some day, Gilgamesh set out on the most perilous journey of all, the search for immortality. In the course of his search, Gilgamesh endured a disastrous world flood, battled deadly serpents, and even crossed the Waters of Death—but he failed to find the secret of eternal life.

The tale ends with Gilgamesh back at the gates of Uruk. As he views the greatness of this city, with its high walls and beautiful masonry, he notices that at the base of the gates is a stone tablet on which the story of his exploits has been carved. Gilgamesh finally realizes that this is the only immortality he will ever achieve and gives up his quest.

opposite
This relief from the temple of Sargon II, eighth century B.C., represents King Gilgamesh. This Sumerian hero, described as "two-thirds god and one-third man," gave up the peace and prosperity of his kingdom to go off in search of adventure and the secret of eternal life.

right
The Sultan Schahriar, engrossed in Scheherazade's delightful story, decides to let her live until the following night so that she can finish her tale.

opposite
Many of the stories from The Arabian Nights *are about the exploits and adventures of young princes. In the "Third Kalandar's Tale," for example, the hero-prince survives a sinking mountain, a booby-trapped island, and a scorching desert before losing one eye saving forty princesses trapped in a monster-infested palace.*

The Thousand and One Nights
A Collection of Arabian and Persian Tales

There was once a sultan named Schahriar who had a wife whom he loved more than anything in the world. His greatest happiness was to lavish her with gifts of the finest dresses and the most dazzling jewels. It was therefore with the deepest shame and sorrow that he accidentally discovered, after they had been married several years, that she had been repeatedly unfaithful to him. In fact, her whole conduct during their marriage turned out to have been so bad that King Schahriar had no other choice than to order his grand vizier to put her to death.

So deep was the shock from his wife's betrayal that after much thought the sultan came to the conclusion that all women were as wicked as the sultana, and therefore the fewer there were in the world the better. So he decreed that every evening he would marry a fresh wife and would then have her strangled the following morning by the grand vizier, whose other duty it was to constantly find new brides for the sultan. The poor man, of course, was horrified with his duties, but there was no escape; every day he saw a girl married and a wife dead.

Needless to say, the people of the kingdom were shocked at this state of affairs and terrified that their own daughters or sisters who would be chosen as the king's next bride and victim. The grand vizier himself was the father of two daughters, Scheherazade and Dinarzade. Dinarzade was an average young girl, but her older sister, Scheherazade, was not only beautiful but exceedingly clever and very courageous. In addition, as the eldest, she had received a thorough education in philosophy, medicine, history, and the fine arts.

18 Heroes of Egyptian and Middle Eastern Mythology

"Open, Sesame"

One day, Scheherazade told her father that she had a plan to stop the king's barbarous practice of murdering his wives and asked him to let her be the next girl he brought to marry the king. Knowing that he would be the one who would have to kill his own beloved daughter the next morning if the plan failed, the horrified grand vizier asked the girl if she had lost her senses. It took Scheherazade a long time to persuade him that her plan would work. Still, it was with a heavy heart that her father agreed. Then Scheherazade made a pact with her sister Dinarzade. "When his Highness receives me," she said, "I shall beg him, as a last favor, to let you sleep in our chamber, so that I may have your company during the last night I am alive. If he grants me my wish, be sure that you wake me an hour before dawn, and say, 'My sister, if you are not asleep, I beg you, before the sun rises, to tell me one of your charming stories.'" Dinarzade gladly agreed.

When the time came, the king did indeed grant Scheherazade her wish and Dinarzade was sent for. An hour before daybreak Dinarzade awoke and begged her sister to tell a story, as she had promised. When the sultan gave his permission, Scheherazade began.

Drawing on her great knowledge of history and literature, Scheherazade wove an exciting adventure story about a genie and a merchant but just as the tale had reached a particularly suspenseful moment of climax, the sun came up and she stopped. As planned, her sister cried out, "What a wonderful story!"

"The rest is even more wonderful," replied Scheherazade, "and if the Sultan would allow me to live another day, I could tell you the rest tonight."

King Schahriar, who had been engrossed in Scheherazade's delightful tale, said to himself, "I will wait till tomorrow. After all, I can always have her killed once I hear the end of her story." So the next morning, an hour before sunrise, Dinarzade again woke her sister and begged her to continue the story. Again the sultan agreed.

So Scheherazade went on telling stories. Each tale had a tale within a tale and thus one story led right into another so that she was never really finished. Every morning she'd stop at a point of exciting suspense, and every morning the sultan would let her live one more day to finish it. After a thousand and one nights of this, the sultan finally became so fond of Scheherazade that he gave up the idea of killing her.

THE TALE OF THE FIFTH VOYAGE OF SINBAD THE SAILOR
A Tale from the Thousand and One Nights

When Sinbad was in his late teens he inherited considerable wealth from his parents and, at first, being young and foolish, squandered it recklessly on every kind of pleasure. He came to understand, however, that unless he changed his ways, he would soon be poor and miserable. So he sold all his household goods and joined a company of merchants who had bought a ship and they sailed to sea on a course toward the East Indies by way of the Persian Gulf. (In all, Sinbad made seven such memorable voyages before he finally returned home for good to retire a wealthy man.)

After enduring shipwrecks, hurricanes, snake-infested islands covered with diamonds and emeralds, evil, hairy dwarves, even more evil ogres, man-eating eagles, and an interesting assortment of other dangers and evil creatures, Sinbad returned home from his fourth voyage with a small fortune in spices and precious stones. One would think that everything he had gone through would make him look forward to a quiet life of pleasure and comfort, but he quickly became bored and longed instead for the adventure of a fifth voyage.

This time, he set out with a ship and crew of his own. They set sail with the first favorable wind, and after a long voyage upon the open seas landed upon an uninhabited island which they set out to explore. They had not gone very far when they spotted a huge roc's egg just starting to hatch. In spite of Sinbad's protests, the merchants immediately took their hatchets and smashed the egg, killing the young bird. Then they lit a fire, and as Sinbad watched aghast, they hacked the baby bird to bits and proceeded to roast the flesh. Just as they finished their meal, the air above them darkened with two

left
Whenever Sinbad returned from one of his Seven Voyages, he delighted and amazed his friends with tales of his harrowing adventures with shipwrecks, evil monsters, and lost fortunes of spices and precious stones.

opposite
In another of Scheherazade's tales, "Ali Baba and the Forty Thieves," the hero Ali Baba overhears the thieves use the magic words "open sesame" to enter the secret hideaway where they hid their plunder.

huge, ominous shadows. Running in terror, the men managed to make it to the ship and even get the sails hoisted, but before they could build up any speed, the parent birds dropped two boulders on the ship, smashing it into a thousand fragments, and crushing or drowning all the passengers and crew. Except for Sinbad, that is.

Sinbad survived by grabbing a piece of driftwood and floating until, many hours later, he was washed up on the green shores of a strange and delightful island. The lush place was thick with trees laden with flowers and fruit, and there was a crystal stream wandering in and out under their shadows.

As Sinbad started to explore the island, he came upon an old man, bent and feeble, sitting on the riverbank. When he greeted him, the old man made signs that he wanted Sinbad to carry him on his back across the river so he could gather some fruit.

Pitying his age and feebleness, Sinbad picked him up on his back and waded across the stream. But when they reached the other side, instead of getting down, this creature who had seemed to be so feeble and decrepit suddenly leaped quite nimbly up on Sinbad's shoulders and hooked his legs round his neck, gripping him so tightly that the sailor passed out and fell to the ground,

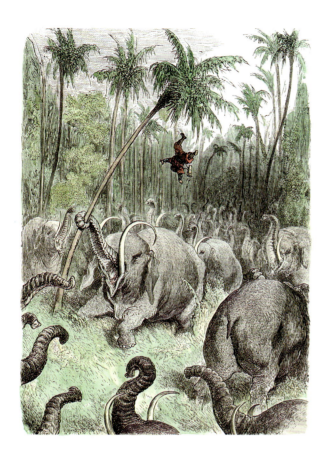

with the creature still wrapped tightly around his neck. When Sinbad came to, the creature prodded him first with one foot and then with the other, until he was forced to get up and stagger about under the trees while the beast on his shoulders gathered and ate the choicest fruits. This went on day after day, all day and all night, until Sinbad was half-dead with weariness.

One day the bored and weary Sinbad happened to notice several large, dry gourds lying under one of the fruit trees. While the creature on his shoulders was busy picking and eating fruit from the tree overhead, Sinbad amused himself by scooping out a gourd's contents and then filling it with the juice of the grapes which grew everywhere around them. When the gourd was full he hid it in the fork of a nearby tree.

A few days later, Sinbad steered the old man toward the same tree and, when he wasn't looking, snatched his gourd and took a long drink from it. The grape juice had fermented into a wine so potent that for a moment Sinbad forgot his detestable burden, and began to sing and dance.

When the old monster noticed how Sinbad was enjoying himself, he stretched out his skinny hand and, seizing the large gourd, first cautiously tasted its contents, then drained it to the very last drop. Soon he too began to sing and after a while, the iron grip of his legs around Sinbad's throat began to loosen. Without a moment's hesitation, Sinbad threw the creature to the ground with such force that he died instantly.

Sinbad, overjoyed to have finally rid himself of this nasty creature, ran back down to the seashore where, by the greatest good luck, he ran into some mariners who had anchored off the island to enjoy the delicious fruits. They helped him celebrate his good fortune and then invited him to sail with them, first to the islands where pepper grew, then to Comari where the best coconuts and aloe wood were found. After that, they dove for pearls and soon had a cargo full of them, all very large and quite perfect.

Loaded down with all these treasures, Sinbad finally returned joyfully to Baghdad, to rest from his labors and enjoy the pleasures his riches could buy. When he told his friends about his adventures on this fateful fifth voyage, they exclaimed in amazement, "Don't you know who that was? You fell into the hands of the Old Man of the Sea, and it's a miracle that he didn't strangle you the way he has strangled everyone else on whose shoulders he perched! Any sailor worth his salt knows better than to ever go near that island!"

Sinbad did not remain home long before he was again overcome with a longing for change and adventure. Soon he would embark on his sixth, and even more amazing, voyage.

left
Often shipwrecked on uninhabited islands, Sinbad miraculously survived hurricanes, snake infestations, and even elephant attacks.

opposite
Sinbad's crew was terrorized by rocs, monstrous birds so huge they fed their young on elephants.

Heroes of Egyptian and Middle Eastern Mythology 23

Aladdin and the Wonderful Lamp
A Tale from the Thousand and One Nights

There once lived a poor tailor who had a son called Aladdin, a lazy boy who would do nothing but play all day long in the streets with other little idle boys like himself. This upset his father so much that he died of grief, but even that didn't make Aladdin mend his ways. One day, when he was playing in the streets as usual, a stranger approached him and introduced himself as Aladdin's long-lost uncle. Aladdin's mother, who had never met her husband's brother, thought she saw a family resemblance in the man and gladly welcomed him into their home.

This stranger was really a notorious African magician; when he learned that Aladdin had been too lazy to bother learning a trade, the false uncle told the mother he'd set up a shop for the boy and stock it with merchandise. Aladdin's mother was overjoyed. Then the magician announced that before the boy began working, the two of them would take a short journey.

The next day, the magician led Aladdin out of the city gates, through some beautiful gardens, and up into the foothills of the mountains. At last they came to a narrow valley between two mountains where the false uncle announced that he had something wonderful to show Aladdin. They built a fire and when it was lit, the magician threw a strange powder into it while he muttered some magical words. The earth trembled a little and opened in front of them, disclosing a square, flat stone with a brass ring in the middle to raise it by.

By this time, Aladdin was scared to death. He tried to run away, but the magician caught him and hit him so hard that he knocked him down. Then his uncle's voice softened and he said more kindly that beneath the stone was a great treasure that would be Aladdin's alone if he did exactly as his "uncle" instructed him. When Aladdin heard the word treasure, he forgot his fears and grasped the ring as he was told. The stone came up quite easily and some steps appeared leading down into a deep cave.

"Go down," said the magician, "and at the foot of those steps you will find an open door leading into three large halls. Go through them quickly and without touching anything, or you will die instantly. These halls lead into a garden of fine fruit trees. Walk on till you come to a terrace where you'll see a lighted lamp. Pour out the oil it contains and bring it to me." Then he drew a magic ring from his finger and gave it to Aladdin for protection.

Aladdin found everything as the magician had said, although he ignored the advice about not touching anything and gathered some fruit off the trees. He found the lamp and started back. Just as he returned to the bottom of the steps, the magician demanded that he throw him the lamp. Now suspecting that the magician might be trying to trick him, Aladdin refused to give it to him until he was out of the cave. Trembling with rage because Aladdin was ruining the plan, the magician threw some more powder on the fire and made the stone with the brass ring roll back into place.

With that, the cunning magician fled, leaving Aladdin trapped within the cave. It was obvious now that he was no uncle of Aladdin's, but an evil thief who had read in his magic books about a wonderful lamp which could make him the most powerful man in the world. The magician's dilemma was that although he alone knew where to find the lamp, he could only receive it from the hand of another. So he had picked out the foolish Aladdin for this purpose, intending to get the lamp and then kill him afterward.

Terrified, Aladdin remained in the dark cave for two days until he accidentally rubbed the magic ring which his false uncle had forgotten to take from him. Immediately an enormous and frightful genie rose out of the earth, saying, "What do you want with me? I am the Slave of the Ring, and will obey you in all things."

Without hesitation, Aladdin cried, "Get me out of here!" In the blink of an eye, he found himself back outside in the sunshine again. As soon as his eyes could bear the light he went home and told his mother what had passed, showing her the lamp and the strange fruit he had gathered in the garden—which turned out to be precious stones.

Aladdin was hungry after his ordeal but his mother had nothing in the house to eat. He looked at the old lamp and figured that if he polished it a bit, he could take it into town and sell it to buy some food. As he began to rub it, a hideous genie appeared and brought them twelve silver plates heaping with delicious food. The boy and his mother sat and ate for a long time. Although she begged her son to sell the lamp because it was obviously possessed by devils, Aladdin decided to keep it as it might prove to be very useful some day. Over the next few years, Aladdin sold the silver plates one by one, and he and his mother lived quite comfortably.

One day Aladdin caught sight of the sultan's beautiful daughter as she rode through town and fell instantly and completely in love. He went home and told his mother that he loved the princess so deeply that he could not possibly live without her, and then asked his mother to go to the sultan, give him the jewels he had brought back from the magic cave, and request his daughter's hand on Aladdin's behalf.

The woman tried for over a week to get in to see the sultan; when she finally did, she told him of her son's all-consuming love for the princess. The sultan wasn't very impressed with her news until she showed him the jewels she had brought. Amazed, the sultan turned to his grand vizier and announced that anyone who placed such value on his daughter should surely be allowed to marry her. The vizier, who wanted his own son to marry the princess, begged the sultan to withhold her hand for three months, in the course of which he hoped his son could come up with a richer present for the sultan. The sultan decided it was good advice and told Aladdin's mother that, though he consented to the marriage, she would have to wait three months before coming back to set the wedding date.

After only two months had elapsed, Aladdin's mother returned one day from the city with the news that the son of the grand vizier was going to marry the sultan's daughter that very night. Aladdin was devastated at first, but

When Aladdin started to polish the old lamp so he could sell it for food, a huge and frightening genie appeared. It cried to him, "Here am I, thy slave and slave to whoso holdeth the lamp!" But the only thing Aladdin could think to wish for was food.

Heroes of Egyptian and Middle Eastern Mythology 25

Although his mother begged him to get rid of the lamp and the evil demons she believed it contained, Aladdin decided to keep it.

remembered the magic lamp and came up with a plan. As before, when he rubbed it a genie appeared asking him what he wished. This time he said that because the sultan had broken his promise and was allowing the grand vizier's son to marry the princess instead of him, he wanted the genie to go to the bride and bridegroom that evening in their bedchamber, kidnap the bridegroom, and make him stand out in the cold all night. The genie obeyed.

The princess passed the most miserable night of her life and by morning was too frightened to speak, even when the genie transported the shivering bridegroom back into her bed. The

26 Heroes of Egyptian and Middle Eastern Mythology

next morning when the sultan greeted his daughter and new son-in-law, the unhappy grand vizier's son jumped up and hid himself while the princess just sat there and sobbed. When the same thing happened on the second morning, the sultan threatened to cut off his daughter's head if she wouldn't tell him what was wrong. Finally she told him. By this time the bridegroom, even though he claimed he dearly loved the princess, announced that he'd rather die than go through another night like that—he wanted an annulment. The sultan gladly granted his request.

When the three months were over, Aladdin's mother once again petitioned the sultan, and this time he decided he was willing to let Aladdin marry his daughter—that is, if he came up with forty gold bowls heaped with jewels and delivered to him by eighty slaves. Aladdin's mother figured that made it hopeless, but Aladdin wasn't worried a bit. He simply rubbed the lamp, summoned the genie, and arranged for the slaves and bowls of jewels.

Before they were wed, Aladdin had the genie build the princess a palace of the finest marble set with precious stones, with velvet carpets, and a domed gold and silver hall in the middle. When the princess finally met Aladdin on the day of their wedding, she was charmed at the sight of him. Love had truly changed Aladdin: the idle boy had grown into a fine handsome man who adored the princess and treated her with kindness and respect. They were very happy in their new palace. By this time, Aladdin had also won the hearts of the people for his courage and kindness.

Aladdin's fame eventually spread as far away as Africa, where the magician was living. When he realized that Aladdin, instead of perishing miserably in the cave, had not only escaped but had married a princess and was living with her in great honor and wealth, he knew immediately that the poor tailor's son could only have accomplished all this by means of the magic lamp. One day when Aladdin was off hunting, the magician dressed as an old street merchant offering to trade new lamps for old ones. His trick worked and a servant at the castle gave him the beat-up old lamp that only Aladdin knew had magical powers.

The magician commanded the genie to transport the castle (with the princess in it) to Africa. When Aladdin returned and saw what had happened, he knew the only person evil enough to do such a thing was the magician, and he set out to find him. With the help of the genie of the ring, he found the palace, and after a joyful reunion with his wife, they plotted how they could kill the magician and get back the lamp.

The princess put on her most beautiful dress and invited the magician to have dinner with her. When he wasn't looking, she slipped some poison Aladdin had brought with him into the lecherous old man's wineglass. When the magician drained his glass and fell back lifeless, the princess let Aladdin in and he took the lamp from the dead magician's vest. Taking the princess by the hand, he commanded the genie of the lamp to transport them and the palace back to the sultan's kingdom.

When Aladdin told the sultan what had happened, and showed him the body of the magician as proof, the overjoyed sultan proclaimed a ten-day feast in his honor. Aladdin had many more adventures, which are related in other tales of the *Thousand and One Nights*.

Chapter 2

Heroes of Classical Greek Mythology

Greek mythology, which can be traced back to before 1000 B.C., is based on a complicated hierarchy of major and minor divinities ruled over by Zeus, King of the Olympian Gods, and his wife, Hera. Under them were various lesser gods and goddesses such as Poseidon, God of the Sea, Athena, Goddess of War and Wisdom, and Hermes, the Messenger of the Gods as well as the God of Thieves and Moneymakers. Next in order of power came the minor divinities such as the River Gods, the Muses, and the Fates.

Heroes such as Achilles, Ajax, and Heracles were considered almost as important as the gods themselves, even though they were not as powerful. A hero was usually the offspring of the union between a god and a mortal.

The Romans took over the Greek gods pretty much in their entirety, although they did change most of the names, giving the Greek gods the names of preexisting Roman deities (which made things pretty confusing for many Romans at first).

2

Perseus, Slayer of Medusa

After an oracle prophesied that his own grandson would one day kill him, King Acrisius of Argos locked his only daughter, Danaë, in a bronze tower to prevent her ever having children.

The poor girl, locked in the tower for eighteen years, grew into a beautiful young woman. One summer afternoon a shower of gold streamed through the tower's only window and magically turned into a handsome god with a thunderbolt in each hand. He was Zeus, and he had come to make Danaë his lover.

He didn't have the power to free her from the tower, he said, but he could transform her horrible prison into a sunny, flower-filled meadow. When the handsome young god kept his promise, Danaë agreed to lie with him, and they lived happily in their meadow home for over a year. But when King Acrisius saw a mysterious, radiant light coming out of his daughter's small tower window, he became suspicious. He had his men rip a hole in one of the walls, then climbed up into the tower to inspect for himself. To his horror, he saw his smiling daughter Danaë with a baby on her lap. Furious, he immediately had his men lock Danaë and baby Perseus up in a large chest and cast them out to sea.

Somehow mother and son managed to get safely to the island of Seriphus where Polydectes was king. The king's brother, who was a fisherman, caught the chest in his net and pulled them to shore. Unknown to King Polydectes, Perseus grew up on the island to become a strong young man and a soldier in the king's army.

One day, King Polydectes was riding through his kingdom and caught a glimpse of the still-beautiful Danaë. He immediately declared his intention of marrying her; as he was a repulsive old man, she rejected him. If Perseus hadn't been there to protect her, the outraged king would have forced her to marry him anyway. It didn't take King Polydectes long to come up with a plan to get rid of Perseus. It was the custom in the kingdom for everyone to give the king a present when he announced his engagement, so he pretended to be marrying another woman, knowing that Perseus was too poor to buy him anything. When Perseus arrived at the engagement dinner empty-handed, Polydectes acted furious, calling the boy lazy and worthless.

As the king had predicted, the proud and hot-tempered youth declared, "I can bring you any present in the world! *Anything*, only name it!" "Bring me the head of the gorgon Medusa," replied Polydectes. Although it was common knowledge that all the men who had tried before had not lived to tell about it, Perseus readily agreed.

opposite
Greek heroes have remained popular subjects for artists long after the decline of Greek civilization. In this seventeenth-century painting, Perseus and Andromeda, *Italian painter Giuseppe Cesari shows the winged Perseus rescuing the beautiful Andromeda, who has been chained to a rock.*

30 Heroes of Classical Greek Mythology

Heroes of Classical Greek Mythology 31

For weeks Perseus wandered around the countryside searching for the lair of the gorgons without success. Finally one night, tired and hopelessly lost, he was overcome with despair. Even if he ever found the gorgons, he knew the idea of killing them was nearly hopeless. They were hideous monsters with black serpents writhing on their heads instead of hair and brass hands that could squash a man as if he were a mere mosquito. And most deadly of all, they were so ugly that anyone who looked at them immediately turned to stone.

Suddenly a tall woman and a young man with winged sandals appeared at his campsite. The man said, "I am your brother Hermes and this is our sister Athena. We know that you too are a son of Zeus and we've come to help you slay Medusa." They gave Perseus the winged sandals, a magic sickle, and a shield to reflect the image of the gorgon so he wouldn't be turned into stone. Before they disappeared, they told him how to find the Nymphs of the North, the only creatures who could tell him how to get to the gorgons' lair.

The kindly Nymphs of the North not only gave Perseus directions, they gave him the Cap of Darkness (which has the power to make its wearer invisible) and a magic wallet.

The next morning, Perseus traveled north until he found the gorgons' island; their lair was surrounded by eerie stone statues that used to be live men. He raised his shield and in its reflection saw that Medusa and her sisters were asleep. He put on the Cap of Darkness and crept down to them. Before the sisters could awaken and defend themselves, Perseus furiously swung the magic sickle until he could feel it tearing through the bone and sinew of Medusa's neck. Still careful to look only at the reflection in his

shield, he took Medusa's severed head and carefully wrapped it in the magic wallet. Suddenly Medusa's sisters woke up and attacked Perseus, but he flew quickly out of their reach.

Perseus had several exciting adventures on his way back to Seriphus with the gorgon's head. He came across the titan Atlas struggling under his burden of holding up the sky. Perseus took

pity on Atlas, and to release him from the terrible weight of his burden, showed him Medusa's head and turned him into stone.

Next Perseus came upon a girl named Andromeda chained to a rock at the edge of the sea. Her mother had boasted that the girl was more beautiful than the Nereids, which so angered Poseidon, god of the sea, that he ordered Andromeda sacrificed to a sea monster. Just as the monster rose from the sea, Perseus swiftly pulled Medusa's head out of the wallet and turned the creature to stone. He cut Andromeda's chains and took her to her father, King Cepheus of Phoenicia, who was so grateful for the return of his daughter that he granted Perseus Andromeda's hand in marriage.

The snake-haired gorgon Medusa, depicted here in a painting by Peter Paul Rubens, The Head of Medusa, *was so hideous that anyone who looked directly into her face was immediately turned to stone.*

Heroes of Classical Greek Mythology **33**

Perseus continued his journey back to Seriphus in the company of his new wife until they reached Larissa, where Perseus wanted to compete in an athletic competition that was being held. That afternoon, however, when Perseus threw a discus, he accidentally hit and killed an old man up in the stands. The old man was none other than his grandfather, King Acrisius. The prophecy had come true.

Perseus and Andromeda lived happily and ruled the kingdom of Argos well for many years. A number of their descendants became great heroes and kings; perhaps the greatest of these was Heracles, the strongest man in the world.

Theseus and the Minotaur

Theseus was the son of King Aegeus, but his father had left his mother, Aethra, before he was even born. His mother raised him to manhood by herself in a small town called Troezen. Just before Aegeus left, he said to Aethra, "If we have a son, when he is old enough and strong enough, tell him to lift this rock and take my sword and sandals from under it." Then King Aegeus placed his sword and sandals under a large boulder and set sail for Athens.

Theseus grew into a remarkably strong young man. One day, Aethra took him to the large boulder and told him to try to lift it. Theseus wrapped his arms around the huge boulder and lifted it as easily as if it were an empty basket, and tossed it into a nearby forest. Aethra told him that he was to take the sword and sandals and go to Athens to visit his father.

After a number of adventures with thieves and giants along the way, Theseus arrived at the palace in Athens. He was happy and excited at the prospect of meeting the father he had never known. He did not know that Aegeus had been tricked into marrying a sorceress named Medea. With her evil powers, Medea knew exactly who Theseus was as soon as he reached the outskirts of town. She was also smart enough to know that Theseus would try to get rid of her when he realized how she had tricked his father. So she devised a plan.

Medea told Aegeus that this young man had come to kill him and the best way to outwit him was to invite him in and then slip him some poisoned wine. Aegeus, not knowing that Theseus was his own son, agreed and immediately sent his couriers to invite Theseus to a special banquet. When all the guests were seated, King Aegeus proposed a toast. Just as Theseus was about to drink his wine, Aegeus recognized the sword he was wearing and dashed the goblet of poison to the floor. In that instant, the spell Medea had cast over the king was broken. Theseus and Aegeus were overwhelmed with joy at their reunion and as they talked happily long into the night, Medea made her timely escape in a chariot drawn by dragons. No one missed her.

There was great joy in Athens for many months until the day a large ship with black sails approached the harbor. The eldest son of King Minos of Crete had been accidentally killed while he was in Athens and the angry king was demanding retribution. Seven young men and seven young women from Athens were to be shipped to Crete every year to be sacrificed to the man-eating Minotaur, a creature half man and half bull. He lived in the Labyrinth, a large maze of tunnels from which no mortal had ever escaped.

Angry and horrified, Theseus went to Aegeus and demanded to be sent to Crete as one of the victims so he could slay the beast. At first Aegeus refused to let his beloved son and heir risk such an adventure, but finally he gave his reluctant approval. Before Theseus left, his father made him promise that if he returned alive, he would change the sails on the ship from black to white before it reentered the Athenian harbor.

As soon as Theseus and the thirteen other victims landed on Crete, King Minos paraded them through the city on their way to the Labyrinth. One of the spectators lining the streets to watch the Athenian victims was Ariadne, the beautiful daughter of King Minos; she fell in love with Theseus the moment she saw him.

That night, she sent in secret for Daedalus, the royal architect who had designed the terrible and deadly Labyrinth, and demanded that he show her a way to escape from it. He did and she immediately sent for Theseus and told him she would help him escape if he promised to marry her afterward and take her back to Athens with him. Theseus gladly made this promise to the beautiful Ariadne and she showed him the trick she had learned from Daedalus: to take a ball of thread with him, tie it to the door as soon as he entered the Labyrinth, and then unwind it as he roamed through the Labyrinth's tunnels.

As planned, the next day Theseus and the others were forced into the Labyrinth. Theseus tied the string to a rock near the entrance and told his thirteen companions to stay close and follow him. After many hours of frustrating twisting and turning, he led them to the center of the Labyrinth where the Minotaur lay sleeping. Theseus had only his fists with which to fight the beast, but without hesitating he jumped on him and ripped off one of his long spiked horns. He took the horn and started poking the Minotaur with it; by this time, the beast was pawing and snorting with rage. Theseus ran to a safe distance and threw the horn like a javelin—it ripped through the monster's neck and killed him instantly.

His companions cheered their new hero as they followed the thread back to the Labyrinth's

Before the terrifying Minotaur could slaughter and eat the youths, Theseus grappled the beast and ripped off its horn.

Heroes of Classical Greek Mythology 35

After slaying the Minotaur, Theseus led his companions back out of the labyrinth to safety. They joined Ariadne and set sail for Greece.

entrance. They met Ariadne at the black-sailed ship and quickly set sail for Athens. One night at sea, the god Dionysus came to Theseus and said, "You mustn't marry Princess Ariadne for I have chosen her as my own bride. Leave her on the island of Naxos."

Theseus reluctantly did as the god told him. Afterward, he was so overcome with sadness that, nearing Athens, he forgot his promise to change the sails from black to white. Old Aegeus had been sitting on a cliff, watching and waiting for Theseus. When the King saw the black sails, he believed his son was dead and he threw himself into the sea in despair. That fatal stretch of water is still called the Aegean Sea.

Theseus went on to become a great king—and to have many more adventures. While having all the traditional heroic qualities such as strength and courage, he also proved to be intelligent and wise.

The Labors of Heracles

Zeus, the most powerful of all the gods, was known to be unfaithful to his wife, the goddess Hera, on a number of occasions with mortal women. One of these mortal women was Alkmene, Queen of Tiryns, who gave birth to a boy named Heracles. He grew up to be the strongest mortal who ever lived and one of Greece's most celebrated mythological heroes.

Hera did not take Zeus's unfaithfulness lightly, however, and was extremely jealous of his mortal children. When she heard that Heracles had been born to Alkmene, she sent two snakes to kill him in his cradle; but to everyone's amazement, the child quickly strangled the snakes with his bare hands.

As he grew up, Heracles was taught the use of weapons by the centaur Chiron, who also trained him to be an excellent sportsman. He was taught the arts of chariot driving, music, and archery by the best teachers in the land. When he was old enough, he married Megara, the daughter of Creon, King of Thebes.

Hera, in the meantime, was not one to simply forgive and forget and she remained Heracles' bitter and sworn enemy. No longer content to kill him, she bided her time until he and Megara had started a small family, and then used her powers to make him go insane just long enough to burn his wife and children alive.

Afterward, when he recovered his sanity, the despairing Heracles suffered terrible agony over what he had done. One day he consulted the oracle at Delphi and begged for a way to atone for his horrifying deed. The oracle ordered him to become the servant of his cousin Eurytheus, King of Argos, who lived in Mycenae and was only too happy to come up with twelve challenging labors for Heracles to complete before he could be forgiven for his crime. Any one of these tasks would have been impossible for a normal human, but Heracles was no average mortal.

The first labor was to kill the lion of Nimea, a beast that no weapon had ever been able to wound. Heracles solved the problem by simply choking the animal to death, then carrying the carcass back to Mycenae on his back.

The second task was to go to the swamps of Lerna and kill the nine-headed creature that lived there—the Hydra. For every head that was chopped off, this monster grew two right back in its place. On top of that, one of the Hydra's heads was immortal and couldn't be killed at all. Heracles used a red-hot brand to sear the creature's neck as he cut off each one, preventing it from sprouting new heads. Then he chopped off the immortal head and buried it securely under a huge rock.

The third labor was even trickier—bringing back alive the stag with golden horns that lived in the forests of Cerynita. Simply shooting it would have been easy, but catching it alive took Heracles a whole year.

The creature he had to capture for his fourth task was a great boar that had its lair on Mount Erymanthus. This, too, required a long time because he had to chase the beast from place to place until it was exhausted. He finally managed to trap it by driving it deep into a snowbank.

For the fifth task, Heracles was supposed to clean the Augean stables in a single day. Augeas had thousands of cattle and his stables had not been cleaned in many, many years—this was truly an overwhelming task. But Heracles came up with an ingenious and effective plan: he diverted the courses of two rivers and made them flow through the stables in a great flood that washed out the filth in no time at all.

In his final labor, Heracles wrestled the fierce three-headed dog Cerberus who guarded the gates of the underworld.

Heroes of Classical Greek Mythology 37

Heracles borrowed a rattle from the goddess Athena to complete his sixth labor. His task was to drive away the enormous number of brass-clawed, man-eating birds that had been plaguing the people of Stymphalus. He frightened the birds out of the marsh with Athena's rattle (which was filled with dried dragon's eyes) and then shot them dead as they flew with his poisoned arrows.

Heracles's seventh labor was to capture the mad, fire-belching bull that was terrorizing the people on the island of Crete. He captured it single-handedly, then heaved it across his shoulders and carried it to a ship that would take it back to King Eurytheus.

The eighth labor was to capture the wild horses of Diomedes, which ate human flesh. To do this, Heracles first killed their owner, Diomedes, then subdued the horses by feeding them Diomedes's flesh. He carried them back on his shoulders to his cousin.

The ninth labor was to bring back the girdle of Hippolyta, Queen of the Amazons. At first it seemed that this would be an easy task; when Heracles arrived, Hippolyta treated him kindly and even agreed to give him the girdle. But Hera, who still hadn't forgotten her bitter grudge, stirred up trouble by making the fierce Amazon women believe that Heracles was really there to carry off their queen. When they charged his ship, he immediately assumed that Hippolyta had put them up to it, and, without any hesitation at all, killed her. He somehow managed to fight off the others long enough to seize her girdle and sail away.

Heracles's tenth labor was to capture yet another monstrous creature—the "cattle of Geryon"—an animal with three bodies that lived on the island of Erythia. To do that, he first had to kill the giant Erytion and the giant's two-headed dog.

The eleventh labor made the ones before it look easy. Heracles was simply supposed to bring back the golden apples of the Hesperides (nymphs), but he had no idea where to even look for them. Finally, he asked Atlas, the father of the Hesperides, to help him. Atlas, who carried the world upon his shoulders, agreed to get the apples for Heracles if Heracles took up the heavy burden for him while he did so. Atlas quickly found the apples, but then, seeing a chance to rid himself of his heavy task forever, refused to take the world back again. He said he'd bring the apples to Eurytheus himself. Atlas might have actually gotten away with it if he'd been a little smarter. Heracles pretended to agree to the plan on the condition that Atlas could just take the burden again for a minute or two while Heracles found a good cushion for his shoulders. Of course the minute Atlas took the world back on his shoulders, Heracles left with the apples.

The twelfth labor was the worst of all. Heracles was to descend to Hades, the underworld, and bring back Cerberus, the three-headed watchdog that guarded its gates. He finally managed to wrestle the monstrous dog into submission and then carried it all the way up to earth and back to Mycenae where he wearily presented it to Eurytheus. The king, however, was so terrified of the animal that he hid in a large jar and demanded that Heracles take it back to Hades immediately. Heracles did just that, and it proved to be his last labor. Through his incredible efforts, he had earned his freedom and had atoned for his terrible deed.

opposite
This 1580 painting by Bartholomaeus Spranger shows Heracles carrying his wife Deianeira away from the dead centaur Nessus, whom Heracles has killed for trying to rape her. Nessus did have time to give Deianeira a potion he said would help her keep her husband's love forever; but it was really a terrible poison that destroyed Heracles' body as it killed him.

Heroes of Classical Greek Mythology

A Difference in Philosophy

The Greeks and Romans may have shared the same gods, but they looked at life from two very different perspectives. Greek mythology, like Greek society, valued individualism and differences in personality and character. Greek civilization was conducted mostly from small, self-governing city states. The Greeks loved life but did not believe in any sort of heavenly existence after death. They believed that the afterlife, even for the greatest of men, would be an eternity of unpleasantness, or at the very least of boredom. The only sort of positive eternity that a man could achieve came by performing great deeds that would be remembered after his death.

The Greeks were very aware of the contradiction that the very virtues that make a human being great are often those that can also lead to his or her undoing. As a result, their gods and heroes were depicted with both strengths and weaknesses. They accomplished great deeds, but they also made mistakes, and their pride, jealousy, and greed often got them into trouble. Heracles, for example, was known to mistreat women. But gods and heroes could also be brave, wise, and compassionate. By defying the gods, it was the heroes who enriched the lives of mankind.

But even though a hero was usually the offspring of a mortal parent and a god or goddess, he was rarely allowed to reach the stature of a god himself, no matter how great his deeds.

The Romans, on the other hand, developed a much more disciplined, less imaginative culture. They valued power, war, and engineering much more than the Greeks did and maintained a vast empire for centuries.

There were two other significant differences between the Greeks and the Romans that colored the myths of their gods and heroes. The average Roman was willing to put up with more hardships and less freedom in this life because he or she believed that there would be a better life in the next world after death. Romans also believed that if a hero (whether all mortal or just half mortal) were powerful enough, he could become a god, an option several Roman emperors decided they were entitled to take.

opposite
Abandoned by her father because she wasn't born a boy, the beautiful Atalanta nevertheless grew up to be as able an archer and hunter as any man in the land.

The Huntress Atalanta

One year, during the annual sacrifice to the gods, King Oeneus of Calydon somehow managed to forget Artemis. The angry goddess responded by unleashing on his kingdom the largest, most savage boar ever seen. The boar quickly destroyed all the crops, killed many men and livestock, and drove the people off the land to the protection of the city walls. It became obvious that they would soon starve if someone didn't get rid of the boar.

Offering the boar's skin as the prize, King Oeneus sent word out imploring the bravest hunters in the kingdom to come forth and try to kill the beast. Heroic hunters from far and wide soon responded to the call, including the king's son, Meleager, and several other famous Argonauts. It was an impressive group and the hunters were excited about getting started on the hunt until a woman, Atalanta, showed up to join them. In spite of Atalanta's superior shooting skills, none of them wanted a woman in the group. When Meleager finally stepped in and

40 Heroes of Classical Greek Mythology

forced the rest of the hunting party to accept Atalanta, they immediately suspected he did it because he was in love with her. It never occurred to them that Meleager might simply have been impressed with her hunting skills.

For Atalanta, this sort of rejection was not a new occurrence. Her father, King Iasus, had been so disgusted she wasn't born a boy that he ordered her carried into the woods and abandoned. But Atalanta didn't die like her father wished. Instead she was adopted by a mother bear who raised her to be strong and tough and to love the outdoors. As she grew up she began to spend time with the hunters who roamed the woods and soon became an expert shot herself.

By the time she was sixteen, Atalanta was as good as or better than any of the Argonauts, but Jason didn't want any women in his outfit. She was also strikingly beautiful, but had no interest whatsoever in getting married, especially after an oracle foretold of a marriage that would end in disaster.

The Calydonian boar hunt started off badly. When the hunters finally found the animal, he attacked them first, savagely killing Ancaeus and several of the others. Peleus threw a javelin at him but ended up hitting his friend Eurytion instead. No one, it seemed, could wound the beast. Eventually it was Atalanta who turned the battle around by drawing first blood with one of her well-aimed arrows. Amphiaraus wounded him again, then Meleager closed in on the boar and finished him off.

But instead of celebrating the death of the beast that had caused so much destruction, a quarrel broke out over whether or not Atalanta deserved the prize of the boar's skin. When it was over Meleager and several of his uncles lay dead.

Heroes of Classical Greek Mythology 41

At the traditional funeral games that were held to honor those who had died in the hunt, Atalanta amazed her fellow hunters even more by beating the legendary Peleus in a wrestling match. Her skills and victories soon became so famous throughout the land that her father forgave her for not being born a boy and told her to return home. He immediately decided that he needed to fulfill his fatherly obligations by finding his daughter a suitable and (of course) rich husband.

Still frightened and suspicious of her father, Atalanta knew that to simply refuse to get married would make the man dangerously angry. Instead she proposed a test. To win her hand, she declared, a suitor would have to beat her in a footrace. Furthermore, losers would be promptly beheaded. Because Atalanta was one of the fastest runners alive, this worked for quite some time. To be fair, though, she always gave her suitors a head start and often wore armor while she ran to even out the odds. Even so, the heads quickly stacked up. Many suitors were willing to risk death to win Atalanta's hand.

One day, a young man named Melanion fell hopelessly in love with her. He knew that he was not fast enough to win the race, so he prayed to Aphrodite, the goddess of love, for help, promising sacrifice and eternal devotion in return for her assistance. Taking pity on Melanion,

42 Heroes of Classical Greek Mythology

with him. Atalanta gave him a good head start, but soon caught up to him anyway. As she approached, he turned and tossed the first of the three apples at her feet. The sight of the magic golden apple was irresistible and she stopped running to pick it up, confident that she could easily make up the time. Soon enough, she was once again catching up with her opponent. Melanion threw the second golden apple, this time further to the side. Again, Atalanta lost time retrieving the apple, and when she caught up to Melanion the finish line was very near. Stopping to chase the third golden apple cost her the race.

To her great surprise, Atalanta discovered that marriage was not that bad after all. Melanion was a gentle and loving husband. But his happiness and joy were so great that he completely forgot his promises of devotion and sacrifice to the goddess Aphrodite. He forgot what terrible fates befall mortals who forget to give proper thanks to the gods. Thus, it's really no wonder that Aphrodite became angry and turned Melanion and Atalanta into a pair of magnificent lions.

Atalanta could have won the race easily if she had not stopped to pick up the golden apples Aphrodite had given Melanion to distract her.

Aphrodite presented him with three golden apples and a plan to win the race.

When Melanion ran his race with Atalanta, he secretly carried the golden apples

Heroes of Classical Greek Mythology 43

Chapter 3

Heroes of the British Isles

The myths and legends of the British Isles come mainly from the ancient Celtic and Anglo-Saxon cultures. The Celts probably arrived in England around 400 B.C., and their influence is most clearly apparent in the long, romantic fairy tales and hero legends of Scotland, Ireland, and Wales.

The Angles and the Saxons conquered Britain in the fifth and sixth centuries A.D. The influence of Anglo-Saxon culture can especially be seen in Old English epic poems such as Beowulf.

Until the seventh or eighth century A.D., the rich mythology and folklore of the British Isles was handed down only by word of mouth, but in the early seventh century, monks in Canterbury started to write down what they knew of Anglo-Saxon history and culture.

In 1066, a Norman named William the Conqueror invaded England and established a rule that was almost entirely Norman-French, greatly changing English life and culture. Many of the ideas of chivalry and knighthood that developed during this time were woven into existing Celtic and Anglo-Saxon tales, creating legends such as King Arthur and his Knights of the Round Table.

3

The Celtic Legends of Ireland

opposite
The rich mythology of the British Isles is the result of numerous conquests and invasions. In 1066, a Norman named William the conqueror crossed the English channel, killed Harold II, the last of the Anglo-Saxon kings, and crowned himself King of England. These events are depicted in the eleventh-century Bayeux tapestry.

below
The warlike Celts who inhabited Ireland before the fourth century B.C. developed myths of epic battles, disastrous floods, and invasions.

Although many Celtic myths and legends were started centuries before the birth of Christ, they had their roots in an oral tradition and were only written down much later, in books such as *The Book of the Dun Cow* (written in the eleventh century), *The Book of Leinster* (twelfth century), *The Book of Ballymote*, *The Yellow Book of Lecan* (fourteenth century), and *The Book of the Dean of Lismore* (fifteenth century).

The first cycle of legends deals only with the age of the gods, primarily recounting their battles with the evil Fomorians of the Land Under the Sea. The exploits of mortal heroes such as Finn MacCool (also sometimes known as Fionn MacCumhall), the Fianna, and Cuchulain are recounted in the subsequent "Fenian" cycles. These detailed stories cover every aspect of the heroes' lives, including births, elopements, adventures, voyages, battles, feasts, courtships, visions, invasions, destructions, expeditions, sieges, dragon-slayings, and, of course, violent deaths.

Finn MacCool and the Fianna of Erin

Some of the most romantic and colorful of the Celtic legends are the stories about the hero Finn MacCool and his elite band of fighting men, the Fianna. The Fianna's main function was to uphold order within Ireland. During the summer months the men lived entirely outdoors, hunting and fishing for food and sport when they weren't off doing their heroic deeds. It was considered a great honor to be a member of the Fianna, and the entrance requirements were far from easy. First of all, a man had to be versed in the *Twelve Books of Poetry* and had to prove he was a man of culture. He also had to pass a number of rigorous initiation rites that tested his superior athletic ability, his skill as a warrior, and his courage.

The leader of this perfect band of warriors, Finn MacCool, was not considered the strongest or most skilled of the Fianna, but he was the truest, wisest, kindest, and most trusted of them.

46 Heroes of the British Isles

He was not just the leader of his people, he was a poet and magician, the pinnacle of achievement for a Celtic warrior. The cycle of legends start with the story of how Finn came to power.

Finn and the Salmon of Knowledge

Originally called Deimne, Finn grew up in the care of two druid women who took him to the wood of Slieve Bladhma when he was ten. Here he was given excellent training in the ways of the warrior. He also spent time with a troupe of poets who taught him the way of words. When he was ready, this fine, good-looking, and highly skilled young lad set out on his own to seek his fortune.

Deimne soon came across a man named Finnegeas who lived by the river Boyne. For seven years Finnegeas had waited on the riverbank, watching for the white-and-red speckled Salmon of Knowledge. He knew that eating this fish would give the first man that tasted it all knowledge. Finnegeas caught the salmon while Deimne was with him and with much joy put it on a spit over an open campfire, entrusting the cooking to Deimne but warning him not to taste it.

After a time, Deimne went to see if the fish was cooked. He couldn't tell just by looking at it, so he touched it with his thumb and promptly burnt himself, leaving a blister. To ease the pain, he put his thumb in his mouth, and thus became the first person to taste the salmon. When Finnegeas looked at the boy's face, he saw the wisdom shining in it, and knew that the salmon was no longer of any use to him.

The boy then gave Finnegeas the fish. After looking at it for a while Finnegeas said to Deimne: "What is your name, boy?" "It is Deimne." he replied. "No, it is not," said Finnegeas. "It was prophesied that someone named Finn would gain the knowledge from the salmon, so your name must be Finn." From that day on, his name was Finn MacCool, and if he needed to know something, all he had to do was put his thumb into his mouth and the knowledge came to him.

opposite
Ireland is a land of mysterious blue mountains, striking rock formations, and windswept moors, an enchanted landscape that almost makes the feats of mythological heroes like Finn MacCool seem plausible.

above
It's said that Finn built this "Giant's Causeway" so he could walk over to Scotland. The rock in the foreground is believed to be his foot.

Heroes of the British Isles 49

According to Irish legend, coming across the mischievous elves known as leprechauns was considered especially lucky because legend had it that if you could catch them, they would reveal the hiding place of their buried treasure.

The Enchanted "Otherworld"

Whether in nursery stories or hero legends, the rich folk literature of the British Isles involved the magical Otherworld in one form or another. In England there were the "drolls," whose devious plots always involved some act of stupidity or cunning. In Scotland there were goblins and witches, bogeys and kelpies, and strange mermen and mermaids who lived in a land beneath the sea. Scotland also had brownies, lovable creatures who were kindly disposed toward people if they were well treated, but capable of terrible mischief if people treated them badly. Ireland and Wales had their faeries and elven "little people." Some Otherworld characters were more evil, like the Irish Lugh, ruler of the Land Under the Sea, or giants with five heads, or wicked stepmothers with enchanted powers. Sometimes the creatures gave heroes help in the form of special skills or knowledge. Sometimes they were minor obstructions the hero had to outwit or distractions which threatened to lead him away from his true tasks. Often they were so feared and treacherous that only a true hero could kill them.

Finn Becomes Leader of the Fianna

After tasting the Salmon of Knowledge, Finn traveled to the court of Conn Ceadchathach at Tara for its much-renowned annual November feast. The king was desolate, however. For the last nine years the feast night was no night of celebration. Instead, his citadel was burned down by an Otherworld being called Aillen, who first lulled everyone, including the soldiers, to sleep with its magical harp music. The desperate king promised that if a man came forward who could save Tara from this fate, he would grant such a man whatever he wanted.

Finn offered to stand guard. With the help of a magical spear, he was able to withstand the enchantment. When he heard Aillen's magical

music, he pressed the point of the spear into his forehead—the pain kept him awake. He jumped up to face the monster, who released a blaze of fire from its mouth, but Finn quenched the blaze with his cloak, then cast his spear at Aillen and killed the beast. When he heard the news, Conn Ceadchathach was so grateful that he appointed Finn as leader of Ireland's most elite and powerful army, the Fianna.

Finn's Hound Cousins

Finn was a great hunter of deer and wild pigs and had many hunting dogs. One story tells about the two great hounds, Bran and Sceolaing, who were his favorites. Bran and Sceolaing were not just excellent hunting dogs, however; they were also Finn's cousins.

It all started when the king of the Dal nAraidhe announced that he desired Finn's aunt Uirne as a wife and Finn happily agreed to the marriage. But the king's first wife was not quite so enthusiastic. In her jealousy, she used her limited knowledge of sorcery to turn Finn's aunt Uirne into a dog. Luckily for Uirne, the warrior Luaghaidh Lagha (who had always been enamored of her) rushed to her aid and killed the king and his treacherous first wife.

Uirne immediately regained her shape and in a short time gratefully married her hero, Luaghaidh. There was still a bit of hound in her, however, and when she bore triplets nine months later she also gave birth to two pups. She gave the pups to Finn, who named them Bran and Sceolaing and trained them as hunting dogs.

Bran was Finn's favorite; Finn loved him intensely. Bran and Finn made great noise together at feasts, and whenever any of the Fianna were hungry Bran would go into the forest and bring them their meals. One day, however, when Bran

When Finn MacCool proved he had the courage and magical powers to stand up to the monsters of the Otherworld, the people gratefully honored him as leader of their elite army, the Fianna.

Heroes of the British Isles 51

was yelping impatiently, Finn got angry and struck him on the head with his whip. Bran stared at his master with tear-filled eyes, then wrenched free, and raced to a lake where he drowned himself. Forever after, when Finn heard the baying of a hunting hound, his heart nearly broke.

Finn and the Bad Servant of Lochlan

One of the Fianna's most harrowing battles took place against invaders from Lochlan, the Land Under the Sea where the evil Fomoire dwell. The story begins with the appearance of a somewhat malformed man; with an iron bit he dragged behind him a dilapidated horse so awkward in its walk, it was a wonder the beast did not fall over. The man announced that he was a man of the Fomoire and that his name was Gille-Decair ("Bad Servant"). He told Finn he wanted to become a member of the Fianna. But instead of acting as though he was worthy of the honor, he behaved obnoxiously. First, he insulted some of Finn's men; and then he demanded double wages, claiming that he was a horseman and that horsemen deserved to be paid more than common foot soldiers. Even his horse was nasty: while Gille-Decair talked, the animal set about maiming and killing the horses of the Fianna.

One of Finn's men, Conan, tried to control the man's horse by jumping on it, but immediately found himself hanging on for dear life as the steed reared and bucked. This was, after all, no ordinary horse. It was Aonbharr, the gallant steed of none other than Lugh, evil ruler of the Land Under the Sea. Other men jumped on to try to subdue it when the horse abruptly took off. Fourteen of Finn's men suddenly found themselves galloping off on a journey they had had no intention of starting, with no idea where they would end up. When Finn looked around, Gille-Decair had also disappeared, leaving Finn with the question of how he could possibly save his men.

Drawing on his magical powers, Finn summoned Otherworld aid to help him in his quest. Two men immediately came to help him—with only three blows one of them could create a ship that could hold three thousand men. In these special ships, Finn and his remaining men set off on the tracks of Aonbharr and the fourteen abducted men. For three nights and three days the sea was relentless in its wildness and fury, yet Finn and

Another of the extraordinary rock formations to be found at Giant's Causeway, in Ireland.

52 Heroes of the British Isles

his men carried on as if the waves were mere ripples on a pond.

On the fourth day a huge gray mountain whose slopes were sheer, smooth rock rose out of the sea before them. The mountain was obviously impossible to climb. Then the other man aiding Finn set to work. His special skill was a superhuman ability to scale sheer cliffs. On his way up, he pounded staves into the mountainside to provide footholds, allowing Finn and his men to quickly scale the mountain and rescue the fourteen warriors kidnapped by Lugh's horse Aonbharr.

A stone carving of the head of a Celtic hero.

The Irish Achilles

Another important Irish Celtic hero, Cuchulain, bears a striking similarity to the Greek Achilles, even though Ireland and Greece are at opposite ends of the European continent. Like Achilles, Cuchulain is portrayed as extremely courageous (but reckless), impressively fierce, and unafraid to speak his mind. Even his childhood was remarkable: by the time he was eight he was already known all over Ireland for his skill and courage as a warrior. By the time he was seventeen, Cuchulain was, without question, the best warrior in Ireland. Time after time he went after and killed the fearsome giants and grotesque monsters no one else dared to face. One story tells how he killed a particularly hideous dragon that was terrorizing the countryside by springing up, thrusting his arm down the beast's throat, and ripping out its heart.) But above all, Cuchulain was respected for his honor, loyalty, and passion for the truth, qualities which made him a true Celtic hero.

The Celtic Myths of Scotland

Like the other British Isles, Scotland was also overrun by Celts after 400 B.C. Many Celtic myths are common to both Scotland and Ireland, while others are distinctly Scottish. There are a number of creation myths about gods such as the fearsome one-eyed Cailleach Bheare (also known as Mag Moullach or the Storm Hag), who supposedly shaped the many mountains and lakes of the Scottish countryside by throwing peat and rocks into the sea from

Heroes of the British Isles 53

Ireland. There are also great cycles of tales about heroic mortals who are either transformed by visits to magical islands of the Otherworld or who are aided by superhuman powers in their noble adventures. One such story is about Prince Iain.

the stepmother knew she had to have the magic bird it came from. She put a spell on Iain, saying that until he brought her the Blue Falcon, slimy, brown bog water would constantly run through his shoes.

Celtic Scottish warriors fought with bronze swords and helmets such as this one.

Prince Iain's Adventure

It is told that in ancient times a Scottish king and queen gave birth to a son they named Iain. When the queen died, the king soon took another wife. Meanwhile, Prince Iain grew up to be a handsome young man and an excellent hunter. But one day Iain didn't even see a deer, let alone shoot one, and when he aimed an arrow at the Blue Falcon, all he did was knock a feather out of her wing. He put the feather into his bag and went home. When his evil and jealous stepmother demanded to see what he had killed, Iain showed her the feather. As soon as she saw it,

Prince Iain went off as fast as his cold, wet feet could carry him and walked all day looking for the Blue Falcon. When night fell, he found shelter under a briar bush; then who should pass by but Gillie Martin, the Fox. The Fox told him that the Blue Falcon he was looking for belonged to the Big Giant with Five Heads. He advised Iain to become the giant's servant and volunteer to look after his cows, goats, and sheep. In time, the Fox promised Iain, the giant would trust him to feed his Blue Falcon. Then all he had to do was wait until the giant was away from home and carry her off.

So Iain started to work for the giant, who was soon so pleased with how well he tended the animals that he even gave him his Blue Falcon to look after. One day when the giant was gone, Iain saw his chance and grabbed the bird. He threw open the door and was about to take off when the doorpost screamed and the giant came running home. The giant told Iain there was no way he could ever have the Blue Falcon unless he brought the giant the White Sword of Light from the Seven Big Women of Jura.

So Prince Iain was once again wandering the countryside and once again he met Gillie Martin, the Fox. The Fox took him down to the edge of the ocean where he turned himself into a boat. Iain rode the boat over to Jura where the Big Women lived and offered to be their servant. He told them he was good at polishing steel and gold and soon they trusted him to take care of the White Sword of Light. When the women left one day, Iain grabbed the White Sword and was about to make a run for it when the door frame screamed. The Seven Big Women came running home and took the Sword from him. They told him they'd give him the Sword, but only if he brought them the Yellow Filly of the king of Erin (Ireland). So Iain went back to the shore where he listened to the Fox's new plan.

In Erin, it was the same story. When Iain tried to escape with the king's Yellow Filly, the king demanded that Iain first bring him the daughter of the king of France. In France, however, Iain finally got lucky. He actually managed to get the princess on board his ship and was sailing back to Erin to trade her for the Yellow Filly, when the princess announced that she'd much rather be Iain's wife. Iain thought that was a wonderful idea, but he still needed to get the Blue Falcon to get rid of his stepmother's curse. So the Fox once again helped him come up with still another plan.

When the ship came to the shores of Erin, the Fox changed himself into a woman as beautiful as the king of France's daughter. When the king of Erin saw the lovely maiden, he gratefully gave Iain the Yellow Filly, which Iain quickly

rode back to the princess waiting by the seashore. That night, when the king and his new wife were in bed, Gillie Martin changed back from a beautiful young woman and became the Fox again. He tore the flesh from the king and killed him.

Evil monsters often appeared as malformed or gigantic men.

Next, they all sailed back to Jura. Leaving the princess and the Yellow Filly at the shore, the Fox changed himself into a yellow filly and went with Iain to the house of the Seven Women. When the amazed Women saw the magnificent horse, they gladly gave Iain the White Sword of Light. Iain quickly took the sword back to the shore as all Seven of the Big Women eagerly climbed on the back of the yellow filly and went off riding. That is, until the horse kicked up its hind legs and threw all seven of them over a cliff.

Their next stop was the home of the Big Giant with Five Heads. Here, the Fox changed himself into a white sword, which Iain gave to the giant in return for the Blue Falcon. While Iain carried the Blue Falcon back to the seashore where he had left the princess, the giant was having fun fencing with his new sword, swinging it round his head. Suddenly the sword bent itself and, before the giant realized what was happening, he cut off his own heads—all five of them.

When they finally made it back to the stepmother's house, Iain was especially careful to follow the Fox's instructions so she wouldn't turn him into a tree stump—or worse. Riding the Yellow Filly with the princess of France sitting behind him with the Blue Falcon on her lap, Iain galloped toward his stepmother, the queen. When he pointed the White Sword of Light at her, she magically turned into a bundle of firewood which Prince Iain and the Fox quickly burned to wood ash.

Now Iain not only had the best wife in Scotland, he had a horse so fast that she could leave one wind behind her and catch the wind in front, the magic Blue Falcon to keep them supplied with an endless supply of game, and the magnificent White Sword of Light to defend them all from harm. When Iain and the princess thanked the Fox, he merely smiled, wished them well, and went on his way.

Hero Legends of Wales

The *Mabinogion* is a collection of Welsh tales handed down orally for centuries until they were written down during the thirteenth, fourteenth, and fifteenth centuries. *Mabinogi* means "instruction for young poets" in Welsh. The tales are divided into four main parts: Pwyll, Prince of Dyfed; Branwen, the Daughter of Llyr; Manawyddan, the Son of Llyr, and Math, the Son of Mathonwy. Each part tells of members of the Welsh royal households, their battles, heroic journeys, misfortunes in love, and interactions with the magical and supernatural Otherworld.

Pwyll and Rhiannon

An example from the first part of the *Mabinogion* is about Pwyll and the woman he marries, Rhiannon. When the story opens, Pwyll, the noble young Prince of Dyfed, has already held his own against a number of gods, including Arawn, the King of Annwvyn (hell) with whom he was forced to exchange shapes for a year as penance for killing some of the king's dogs. Near Pwyll's palace was a mound upon which, people believed, one could sit and see visions. One day Pwyll decided to visit this mound, and as he sat on it he saw a beautiful lady in golden robes ride past on a white horse, furiously trying to outride

opposite
After seeing the beautiful maiden Rhiannon ride through the forest on her white horse, Prince Pwyll vows to get rid of her unwanted fiancé Gwawl.

Gwawl, the sun god who obviously wanted to marry her. Pwyll saw her again the next day, and this time she stopped. The two soon fell in love and set about devising a plan to get rid of Gwawl, to whom she was unfortunately already betrothed.

At the feast just before Rhiannon and Gwawl's wedding, Pwyll, carrying a magic bag, showed up disguised as a beggar; he begged Gwawl for food. But no matter how much food was put into the bag, it never became full. Exasperated, Gwawl asked whether it would ever be filled, and Pwyll admitted [it] would not, unless a [ma]n were to stomp [th]e contents of the [bag] with both of his [fe]et. When Gwawl got up and stepped into the bag, Pwyll quickly pulled up the sides, trapping Gwawl within. Gwawl begged for mercy, and Pwyll released him, but only after making [a pro]mise to leave [without] taking revenge. [Once he] left, the wedding feast continued, but this time Pwyll was the bridegroom.

Pwyll took his new bride back to Dyfed where they lived happily and ruled for many years. Some years later, Rhiannon gave birth to a baby boy and there was great rejoicing throughout the kingdom. But on the very night of his birth, while Rhiannon and her women servants slept, the baby mysteriously disappeared. The servants awoke first, and when they found the baby gone, they were terrified. Afraid they'd be punished for allowing the baby to disappear, they decided to make it look as if his own mother had killed and eaten him. They killed a young dog, and laid its bones by Rhiannon, rubbing blood onto her face and hands.

Horrified that she had killed her own child, Rhiannon took on a penance, sitting each day outside the castle, telling passersby the terrible tale, and offering to carry them on her back.

But Rhiannon's wasn't the only baby to disappear. As it happened, the same night Rhiannon was giving birth, another strange birth was taking place nearby. Teirnyon, the lord of Gwent, had a mare that would foal every year on the first of May. And every year, the colt would immediately disappear. Baffled and annoyed by these annual disappearances, Teirnyon had finally taken the mare into his house to let her foal there. She bore a large and beautiful colt, but then there was a terrible racket outside, after which a clawed arm came in through the window and attempted to drag the colt away. Teirnyon jumped up and cut off the arm, and then ran outside to see what was trying to steal his colt. To his surprise, he found an infant boy lying on the doorstep.

Teirnyon and his wife took the child in and after a few months began to see his resemblance to Pwyll. Thinking back on the news of Rhiannon and her punishment, they decided that the boy must be her child. They returned the child to his true parents and Rhiannon and Pwyll were overjoyed. They named their beautiful son Pryderi.

After tricking Gwawl into leaving his own wedding ceremony, Prince Pwyll marries Rhiannon in his place.

The Arthurian Legends

According to the many legends written about him, Arthur was the son of the Welsh king Uther Pendragon. Immediately after his birth, the elves bestowed on him long life, riches, and virtues. His father gave Arthur into the keeping of Merlin the Magician, who later took him to Sir Hector to bring the child up as his own son. When Arthur was only fifteen, his real father, Uther, died.

Arthur could not just take his father's place, he had to prove his right to the throne by pulling out a special sword fixed in a great stone. No one else had been able to budge it. This was the first of Arthur's two magic swords, both called Excalibur. (The other was given to him by the Lady of the Lake. According to the story, her arm appeared above the surface of the lake with the sword in hand. When Arthur took it, her arm disappeared.) Arthur took the throne as king of Britain and waged many battles until he finally conquered Scotland, Ireland, Iceland, and the Orkneys. King Arthur later married Guinevere, a lady of noble Roman family, and they held court at Camelot, on the River Usk in England, near the Welsh border. Around him he gathered many strong and brave knights. Because they all sat as equals about a great round table, they eventually came to be known as the Knights of the Round Table. King Arthur extended his conquests far and wide. One day he was summoned to pay tribute to the Emperor Lucius of Rome; he refused and instead declared war on Rome. He went off to war, leaving the kingdom in the hands of Mordred, his nephew, a decision which proved to be a terrible mistake for the kingdom.

On his way to Rome, Arthur bravely slew the giant of St. Michael's Mount. He finally fought his way to the outskirts of Rome and was about to lay siege to the city when he learned that the traitorous Mordred had seized the kingdom in his absence. Arthur immediately rushed home, and killed Mordred in a great battle. But in that battle, Arthur himself was mortally wounded. According to the legend, however, he didn't die. His body was mysteriously carried to the island of Avalon to be healed, and he is expected to return at some future time and resume his rule.

King Arthur seated his brave and noble knights around a round table so they would all be honored equally.

Heroes of the British Isles 59

After battle, King Arthur and his knights tend to the wounded and dying.

Central to the Arthurian legends is the downfall of Arthur's kingdom, but there are many different versions as to how that was ultimately accomplished. Some say it failed due to the treachery of Mordred. Others show that the treachery was only made possible because of the illicit love between the knight Lancelot and Arthur's wife, Guinevere. There are a great number of other romantic and exciting Arthurian legends, such as those involving the search for the Holy Grail, the Fisher King, how the Lady of the Lake got the magic sword, the rise and fall of Merlin the Magician, and many others.

Was There Really a King Arthur?

Although almost every European country has had a version of the romance of Arthur (and knights of the Round Table such as Lancelot, Gawain, and Tristam), most scholars agree that Arthur first appeared in the fourth book of the Welsh *Mabinogion* in stories about the Lady of the Lake, Bedivere, Kay, and Gawain. But in these stories, Arthur was not a mortal King, but King of Fairyland. Over the years, other stories then attached themselves to the name of Arthur, especially myths of ancient Celtic gods and

Otherworld tales of the supernatural embodied in characters such as Merlin. Later, the Norman knights and poets made Arthur a knight like themselves, even though his stories started long before the age of chivalry. They added details of their own with stories of other knights such as Lancelot and Galahad.

Some historians believe that many of the legends began as fact—that there actually was a hero named Arthur living in Britain in the fifth or sixth century A.D. who gained fame as a leader of the Christian Celts in the wars against the heathen Saxon invaders. After Arthur was defeated and killed in battle, his people then fled to the mountains of Wales and to Brittany, where they told stories of Arthur's valor and goodness.

Many writers have interpreted the Arthurian legends. In the fifteenth century Sir Thomas Malory translated many of these romances from Welsh to English. They appeared as *Le Morte Darthur* (The Death of Arthur), one of the first books to be printed in England. T.H. White's *The Once and Future King* became the basis for the musical *Camelot* (1960) and the animated film *The Sword in the Stone* (1963).

Robin Hood

The Anglo-Saxon songs and legends about Robin Hood and his merry outlaws have been entertaining people for over six hundred years. Some people believe the heroic figure of Robin Hood actually existed; others believe only that he should have. According to the story, during the reign of King Richard I, also known as Richard the Lion-Hearted, Robin was an outlaw living in Sherwood Forest with one hundred tall men, good archers all. Robin and his men robbed from the rich, using part of the spoils they acquired for their food, drink, and clothing, and giving away the rest to the needy poor. They were also staunch defenders of womanhood, and did what they could to make sure that no women were oppressed or molested. Needless to say, Robin Hood and his men were very popular with the common people and a constant annoyance to the ruling elite.

One of the best-known Robin Hood stories is a tale about an archery contest as told by Sir Walter Scott in his book *Ivanhoe*. King Richard was out of the country, fighting in the Holy Land at the head of an army of crusaders, and had left the inept Prince John in charge, when Robin Hood decided to compete for the longbow-shooting prize at a royal archery tournament the prince was holding at Ashby. Had anyone known who he was, Robin would, of course, have been arrested; he came in disguise and refused to give his name. After a number of rounds, the competition was narrowed down to just two archers, Robin and Hubert, a forester in the service of one of the king's nobles.

Although Hubert shot his first arrow of the final round close to the center of the target, Robin pointed out to him that he could have gotten it closer had he allowed for the wind. Then Robin stepped up to the mark and carelessly shot his arrow, making it seem as if he had not even looked at the target before shooting. His arrow was two inches closer to the center than Hubert's had been. Prince John was furious that a stranger was beating one of his own men and yelled to Hubert that he'd better win this or he would make things very hard for him. So Hubert stepped up to the mark, took Robin's advice about compensating for the wind, and hit the target dead center. The crowd roared with delight, rooting for Hubert over this stranger.

above
Will Scarlet, one of Robin's merry outlaws, kills a buck for their evening meal.

opposite
Little John offers encouragement as Robin Hood practices his archery for the Royal Tournament.

The prince mocked Robin, pointing out to him that there was no way he could top Hubert's shot, so he didn't even have to bother to try. Robin simply walked up to the mark and shot his arrow. He also hit a bull's-eye—but he hit his by splitting the shaft of Hubert's arrow right down the middle. The crowd was so flabbergasted they couldn't even cheer. Even Prince John admired the stranger's skill so much that he forgot to dislike him. He declared Robin the winner and gave him all the prizes. He also offered Robin a job as his personal bodyguard, an offer Robin was quick to decline. Although he had beaten Hubert fair and square, Robin Hood gave him half the prize before he disappeared into the lights and shadows of his beloved Sherwood Forest.

Beowulf

When the Anglo-Saxons invaded the British Isles in the fifth and sixth centuries, they brought with them songs about their hero Beowulf. But it was not until the seventh or eighth century that some unknown poet wove the tales into a great epic. The hero, Beowulf, is a courageous Swedish prince who fights three major battles in the course of the tale, all against monsters.

The first part of the poem, the prologue, begins with a history of Danish kings, starting with the funeral of King Shild and leading up to the reign of King Hrothgar, Shild's great-grandson. King Hrothgar has just finished building a lavish hall called Herot and has thrown a gala celebration to honor his army's successes in war. But the joy in his kingdom soon turned to fear and despair: the nighttime singing and carousing of Hrothgar's men angered Grendel, a terrible half monster, half man who lived at the bottom of a nearby swamp. Grendel appeared at Hrothgar's hall later that night and killed thirty of Hrothgar's warriors in their sleep. Then, night after night for the next twelve years, the monster crept into the king's palace to slay more sleeping knights; there was nothing Hrothgar and his advisers could do to stop him.

When he heard about Hrothgar's troubles, Beowulf, prince of the Geats, gathered fourteen of his bravest warriors, and set sail from his home in southern Sweden. Beowulf claimed to be an accomplished warrior with particular success in fighting sea monsters. Hrothgar eagerly promised Beowulf great treasures if he could rid them of Grendel.

Beowulf wasted no time. When Grendel appeared later that night, the prince wrestled the monster bare-handed and tore off the monster's arm at the shoulder. Grendel managed to escape, only to die soon afterward in his muddy lair at the bottom of the snake-infested swamp. Delighted, Hrothgar threw a banquet in Beowulf's honor and rewarded him with treasures while his Danish warriors sang songs in praise of Beowulf's triumph.

What none of them knew was that Grendel had a mother who was a monster even more terrible. In the second part of the poem, Grendel's mother takes her bloody revenge. She arrived at the hall late the next night when all the warriors were asleep and

A page taken from a sixth-century version of the epic poem Beowulf, written in Old English.

64 Heroes of the British Isles

carried off Esher, Hrothgar's trusted chief adviser. Once more, Beowulf went to the aid of the Danes. He and his men tracked the she-monster to a cliff where they saw Esher's bloody head floating on the surface of the swamp below. Beowulf dove to the bottom of the snake-infested muck where he found the monster's lair. After a terrible fight, Beowulf stabbed her with his magical sword, Hrunting, then used his bare hands to wring her neck.

Grateful to Beowulf for purging Denmark of its race of evil monsters, King Hrothgar held one more feast in his honor. In the morning the Geats sailed for home. When King Higlac of Sweden heard how Beowulf had killed both Grendel and Grendel's mother, he proclaimed him a national hero and made him his most trusted counselor. In the beginning of part three, Higlac had died and the Geats had chosen Beowulf as their king. Beowulf reigned wisely; his people lived in prosperity and happiness for fifty years, until a great terror fell upon the land. A thief had stupidly stolen a jeweled cup from the den of a sleeping dragon, and the beast now wanted revenge. The dragon terrorized the kingdom by flying through the night and lighting up the darkness with his blazing breath. It burned houses, men, and cattle to ashes with the flames from his hideous mouth.

When the aging King Beowulf heard that even his bravest warriors were terrified of confronting the beast, he took up his sword and shield one last time and set off to find the dragon's den. When he found the cave, he stood at the entrance and cursed the monster until it rushed out at him, roaring hideously and flapping its glowing wings. Beowulf fought bravely but his strength was not as great as it had been when he fought Grendel many years earlier. He managed to pierce the dragon's scales with his sword, but before it died, the dragon engulfed Beowulf in flames and gashed him in the neck with its poisonous fangs.

His men rushed into the cave. The dragon was dead, but it was too late to save Beowulf. He had fought his last battle. His men built a funeral pyre for him at the top of the cliff, then buried the dragon's treasure alongside Beowulf's ashes. And so the poem ends as it began—with the funeral of a great warrior.

Grendel as Hero

In 1971, superb writer and storyteller John Gardner wrote a book called *Grendel*, in which he told the story of Beowulf from the monster Grendel's point of view. In the original poem, Grendel is a symbol of absolute evil and corruption, a loathsome being whose only feelings are hatred and bitterness toward mankind. In Gardner's version, however, even though Grendel is still a hideous-looking beast "crouched in the shadows, stinking of dead men, murdered children, and martyred cows," the reader begins to identify with his pain, frustration, and his terrible loneliness. Although he's supposed to strike fear into the hearts of man and beast, his inept efforts to do so are often more ridiculous than frightening. For example, when an old ram refuses to run and just stands there laughing at him, Grendel stamps his feet, howls, even throws stones at him, yet still the ram won't budge. So Grendel just stares at him in horror and hisses "Scat!" When Beowulf finally hunts him down and slays him, Grendel's death is a sad and pathetic one.

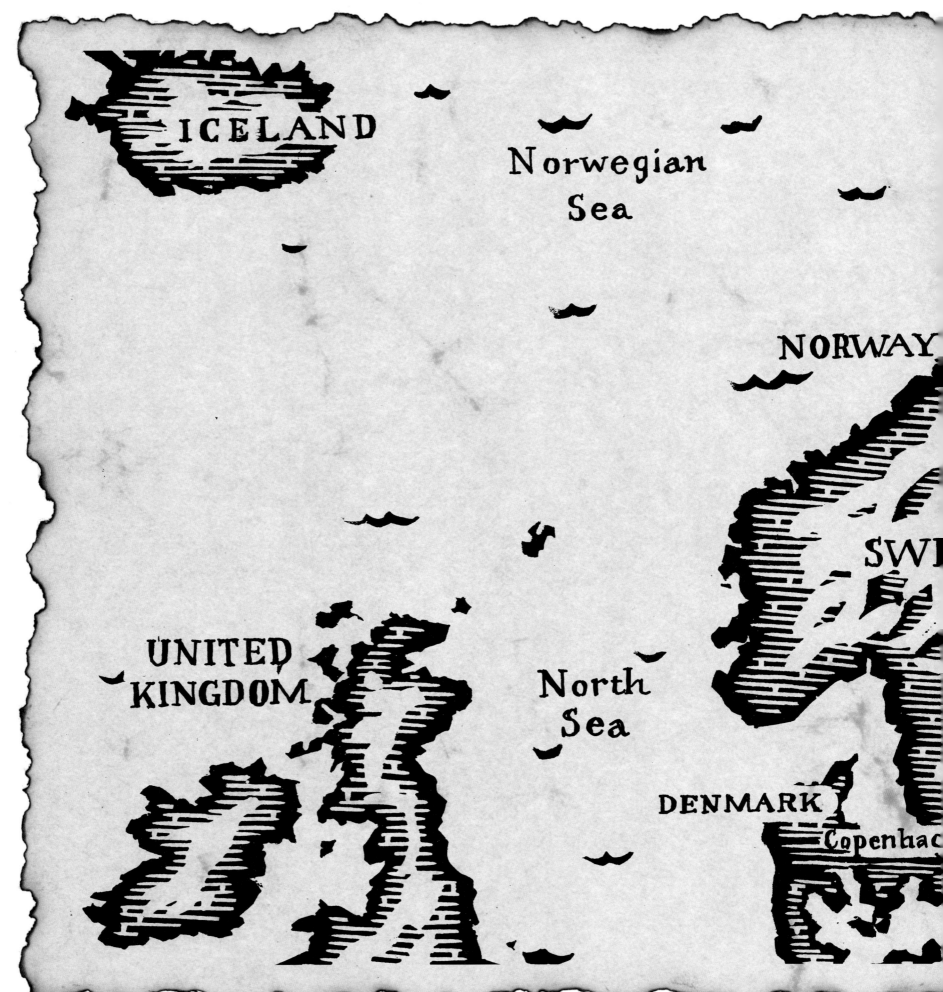

Chapter 4

Heroes of Scandinavian Mythology

The mythology that evolved in the cold lands of northern Europe reflected an endless struggle against ice and cold. The stories of Norse gods and heroes were preserved in two ancient books called the Eddas. The older of the two was written in poem form in the eleventh century (possibly by a writer named Saemund) and consists of fragments about the lives of the Norse gods and two heroic families—the Volsungs and the Nibelungs. The later Edda was written in the early thirteenth century by Snorri Sturluson. Written in prose, this collection was partly a textbook on poetry and partly a chronicling of the Norse gods and their fates.

Long before the myths and legends were ever written down, however, they were kept alive by skalds, traveling poets who made their living reciting the sagas (as the myths and legends were called), primarily at the feasts and banquets of warriors.

4

The Saga of the Volsungs

When Viking warriors died in battle, they were considered heroes and were summoned by the god Odin to his Hall of the Slain, Valhalla. This dead hero is being welcomed into the hall on the back of Odin's eight-legged horse Sleipnir.

The Volsungs were a heroic people descended from the Norse god Odin. The saga begins with the story of Odin's son Sigi, who was declared an outlaw and driven into exile after he murdered another man's thrall (slave). Odin set him up in a new life as king of a place named Hunland. Sigi had a son named Rerir who took the throne many years later. But Rerir was unhappy because he and his wife could not have children. Frigg and Odin heard their prayers and sent a Valkyrie named Ljod to bring them a special apple. Ljod turned herself into a crow and dropped the apple onto the queen's lap; when she ate the apple, she became pregnant. King Rerir died and for six long years the weary queen carried her unborn child, then died in childbirth. She lived just long enough to give her newborn son the name Volsung and kiss him good-bye.

Volsung became the next king of Hunland, and when he grew up he took the Valkyrie Ljod for a wife. Volsung and Ljod had eleven children—a daughter named Signy and ten sons. The oldest and bravest of the sons was Signy's twin brother, Sigmund. The Volsungs were a family of true heroes and were stronger, braver, and fitter than all other men. King Volsung built a palace around a tree and called it Branstock (or Stem of the Children). The trunk of the tree was in the palace and its fruitful boughs stretched out over the roof.

The Hero Sigmund Escapes Siggeir's Treachery

When the Volsung children were older, Siggeir, the mighty king of Gautland (Sweden), decided he wanted to marry Signy. He got her ten brothers to agree to promise him her hand in marriage, even though she wanted absolutely nothing to do with him. At the wedding banquet at

68 Heroes of Scandinavian Mythology

the Volsung palace, an elderly one-eyed man wearing a cape and hood stuck a magnificent sword into the trunk of Branstock and declared that whoever pulled the sword out could have it. (The old man was actually the god Odin in one of his disguises.) Everyone tried, but only Sigmund succeeded. Siggeir was jealous and wanted the sword for himself. He offered Sigmund three times its weight in gold and when Sigmund refused, Siggeir became incensed and immediately began to plot his revenge. Smiling, he invited King Volsung and all of his sons (including Sigmund) to visit him and his new wife, Signy, in Gautland in three months.

The invitation was, of course, just a ruse. Three months later, Volsung and his sons set out on their voyage with three well-manned ships. As soon as they arrived, Siggeir and his army attacked them. King Volsung and his sons fought with great courage, but in the end Volsung was killed and all of his sons taken prisoner. When Signy pleaded with her husband to bind her brothers in stocks out in the forest instead of killing them quickly, Siggeir agreed, since he thought they deserved to be tortured.

For nine nights, Siggeir's mother, a dead sorceress, came back to life in the shape of a she-wolf and ate a Volsung each night until only Sigmund remained. On the tenth day, Signy had her trusted manservant (who had brought her the news) smear honey on Sigmund's face and in his mouth. That night the she-wolf licked the honey and when she stuck her tongue into Sigmund's mouth, he bit it off, killing her. Then Sigmund managed to escape. When Signy heard the news, she went out to find him and convinced him to build an earthen house and hide in the forest. She promised to bring him anything he might need. In the meantime, her brutal husband was celebrating because he thought all the Volsungs except Signy were now dead.

This betrayal sets in motion the first of the saga's many tragic retributions. For years, Signy and Sigmund plotted a way to avenge the death of their father and brothers. Signy had two sons with Siggeir and when the oldest was ten, she sent him to help Sigmund. Sigmund tested the boy's courage by asking him to knead flour, with a serpent in it; the boy would not touch the flour, so Sigmund didn't want him as a helper. Signy told Sigmund to kill the boy, as he was worthless. Sigmund did so. It was the same with Signy's other son.

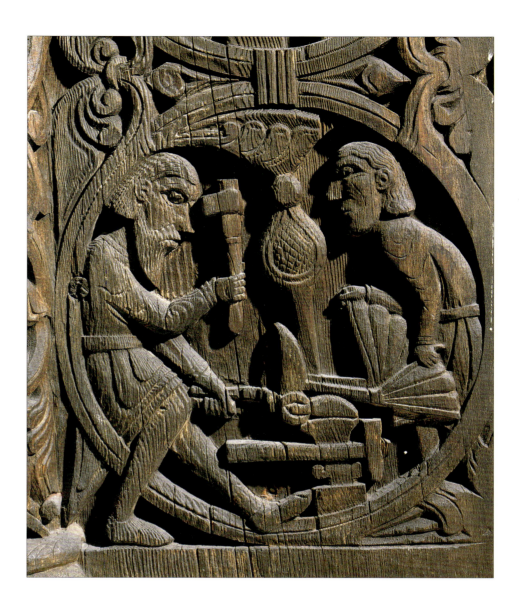

Wooden door panels on a twelfth-century Norwegian church show how Sigurd's sword was reforged so he could go out and slay the dreaded dragon Fafnir.

Heroes of Scandinavian Mythology 69

opposite
Thor, the Thunder God, drove a wagon drawn by goats across the heavens and over mountains to slay his enemies the giants. Known for his awesome strength, fiery temper, and magic hammer, Thor was the most popular—and most feared—Viking deity.

Not a Pretty Bunch

The mythology of the north European countries of Norway, Sweden, Iceland, and Denmark did not have gods of physical strength and beauty like those in Greek and Roman mythology. Odin, the chief god, had only one eye and Tyr, the god of war, had one arm. But then, the Greeks and Romans did not have to struggle against the and cold, or endure rugged landscape, towering mountains, and long, dark winter nights as the Norse did.

The sworn enemies of the Norse gods were a terrible race of evil frost giants. Another class of beings, inferior to the gods but still powerful, were the Elves. The Elves of Light looked like beautiful young children and were kind toward humans, but the Black or Night Elves were ugly, long-nosed dwarves who turned into stone if exposed to light. They possessed knowledge of the mysterious powers of nature and the ability to create magical weapons and tools out of metal and wood.

The gods chose as their home a plain named Ida, where they built the city of Asgard. The chief god, Odin (known in Teutonic legend as Wotan or Woden) was regarded as a war god and the protector of fallen heroes. His magical horse, Sleipnir, had eight legs and was able to gallop through the air and over the seas. Odin was very wise, but the price he paid for that wisdom was the loss of one eye. Some of the many other Norse gods included Thor the Thunderer, who had a magic hammer named Mjollnir; Balder, the beautiful god of light (who was killed by mistletoe, the only thing that could hurt him); Frey, the god of sun and rain; Freyja, the goddess of love and beauty; and Hel, the goddess of death. Loki was the evil trickster, half human and half god.

The gods had made the earth from the body of Yimir, a slain giant. Then they created man from an ash tree and woman from an elm and set them to live in this new place they called Midgard. Heimdal was the keeper of the rainbow bridge over which the gods passed from Asgard to earth.

Unlike most other mythologies, Norse legends did not have happy endings. The Norse gods were deities who knew intense suffering and lived with the knowledge that in the end there would be Ragnarok—a Twilight of the Gods in which they would be horribly defeated by the frost giants. Even mortals had nothing to look forward to. Only courageous warriors who fell in battle went to the heaven of Valhalla. Nevertheless, Norse mythology was based on the belief that heroic action was the highest good. This foreknowledge of doom gave the legends a great sense of tragic nobility.

The Birth of Sinfjotli and Sigmund's Revenge

Signy then got a beautiful sorceress to exchange shapes with her and she went to Sigmund in disguise. After sleeping with him for three nights, Signy returned home and assumed her former shape once more. Some time later she gave birth to Sigmund's child, a large, strong, and handsome boy she named Sinfjotli. When he was old enough, she sent him to Sigmund. Having no idea that Sinfjotli was really his own son, Sigmund put him through the usual tests. Not only did Sinfjotli willingly knead the dough with the live serpent in it, he baked it into bread and was willing to eat it.

When Sigmund finally decided that Sinfjotli was ready, he led him to Siggeir's house to hide in an anteroom and wait for nightfall. In the meantime, two small children of Siggeir and Signy spotted the intruders and ran to tell their father what they had seen. Signy told Sinfjotli to kill them so that they would tell no more tales. He did as she asked him to.

The outraged king gave orders to seize the intruders, and after a long and brave struggle, Sigmund and Sinfjotli were captured and buried alive under a large pile of stones. But with the help of a magic sword that could cut through stone as if it were wood, they escaped. They went straight to the king's hall, heaped wood all around it, and set it on fire. Siggeir was trapped in the hall; when Sigmund called to Signy to escape, she refused. She said that her revenge against Siggeir was complete, and because she had caused her own children to die in the search for that revenge, she now gladly gave up her own life in atonement. Just before she died, she told Sigmund how she had exchanged shapes with the sorceress and revealed that Sinfjotli was really his own son.

Sigmund and Sinfjotli mustered a band of men, commandeered a ship, and set sail for Hunland, the kingdom Sigmund's father, Volsung, had once ruled over. Sigmund took over the government and became a mighty and famous king.

opposite
The German version of the complicated saga of the dragon Fafnir's treasure is often called the Nibelungslied or "Song of the Nibelungs," illustrated here in this nineteenth-century manuscript.

left
This small eleventh-century bronze figure represents the Viking god of fertility and prosperity, Frey. The cult of Frey was popular in Sweden in the Viking age and later spread to Norway and Iceland.

Heroes of Scandinavian Mythology 73

Viking heroes were often buried not only with their helmets and swords, but with all their other possessions, including hoards of gold and silver. This helmet, known as "Sigurd's Helmet," was found in a pre-Viking grave at Vendel, Sweden.

The Death of Sinfjotli

Sigmund's first queen was Borghild of Bralund, with whom he had two sons, Hamud and Helgi Hundingsbane. (Helgi grew up to be a brave and fierce warrior who married a Valkyrie named Sigrun and later died a tragic death. A number of heroic *lays* or stories are written about him.) Unfortunately, it was Borghild who ended up bringing about the death of Sigmund's first son, Sinfjotli.

Sinfjotli proved to be an excellent warrior who spent most of his time engaged in warfare. One day, however, he saw a beautiful woman and fell in love with her. He wanted to marry her, but Borghild had a brother with the same intention. Hatred immediately sprang up between the two rivals, and when Sinfjotli killed her brother, Borghild tried to drive him away. When that

74 Heroes of Scandinavian Mythology

didn't work, she prepared a funeral banquet at which she offered Sinfjotli a large drinking horn in which she had mixed poison. Sinfjotli drank and at once fell down dead.

After burying his son, the enraged and grieving Sigmund drove Borghild away.

The Death of Sigmund

Some years later Sigmund fell in love with Hjordis, the fair daughter of a powerful king named Elylimil, and asked for her hand in marriage. But so did King Lyngvi. Hjordis's father let her decide who she wanted to marry and she chose Sigmund. Not long after, Lyngvi and several of his brothers marshaled their forces and declared war on Sigmund.

Sigmund fought so valiantly that no one was able to stand against him until an old, one-eyed man dressed in a broad-rimmed hat and a blue cloak and carrying a spear in his hands (Odin again) entered Lyngvi's ranks. When Sigmund advanced upon Odin, his great sword broke and the battle took a dreadful turn for the worse. In the end, Sigmund and Hjordis's father, Elylimil, fell, along with most of their men.

The Birth of the Hero Sigurd Fafnirsbane

After Sigmund's death, Hjordis gave birth to his son, Sigurd, a boy who would grow up to be the greatest Volsung of them all. Fearing for their safety, she and her son boarded a Viking ship under the command of Prince Alf of Denmark, who later married her.

Sigurd received his early education in the king's court under the tutelage of a blacksmith, Regin, skilled not only in preparing for warfare, but in sorcery and the reading of magic runes. Regin taught him well.

Regin's story is an interesting one. He had two brothers, Oter and Fafnir, who also had magical powers. Oter often took the shape of an otter because he liked to pass the time catching salmon in a nearby waterfall owned by the dwarf Andvari. The waterfall hid the dwarf's hoard of gold. One day when the gods Odin, Loki, and Hïnir were on a journey, they stopped at the waterfall to rest and saw an otter

Wooden Viking warships like this ninth-century sixteen-seater were sleek and formidable. Dead warriors were often honored with funerals in which they were cast adrift after their ships had been set on fire.

Heroes of Scandinavian Mythology 75

In the Teutonic version of Sigurd's story, his name becomes Siegfried and the treasure is a hoard of gold protected by the Rhine Maidens at the bottom of the Rhine river. While some of the names and details change, however, the plot remains pretty much the same.

feeding on a salmon it had caught. Loki picked up a stone and threw it at the otter, killing it. Taking the pelt with them, the gods stopped at Regin's father's house where they asked for a night's lodging. Regin and Fafnir immediately recognized the otter pelt as their brother and, with the aid of their father, Reidmar, took the gods captive. In fear for their lives, the gods promised the men anything; Reidmar, Fafnir, and Regin decided that they wanted the otter filled with gold. The gods agreed.

The Gold Ring

Not wanting to give up his own riches, Loki immediately started scheming to get the dwarf Andvari's gold to give to Reidmar and his sons. Using a borrowed fishing net, he caught the dwarf and threatened to kill him if he did not immediately surrender his hoard of gold, which included a small but precious gold ring. As the dwarf darted back into the safety of his rocks, he put a curse on the ring and whoever possessed it—starting with the brothers Regin and Fafnir. It didn't take long for the curse to begin taking its terrible effect.

The gods kept their word, filling the otter pelt with Andvari's gold and giving it to the father. When the greedy Reidmar refused to share it with his sons, Fafnir promptly killed him in his sleep and took all the gold for himself. This meant the penniless Regin had to get a job as the king's blacksmith—which was how he became young Sigurd's tutor.

After stealing the gold, Fafnir transformed himself into a huge, venomous serpent and made a lair for himself on Gnita Heath. There he remained, brooding over his hoard of gold.

76 Heroes of Scandinavian Mythology

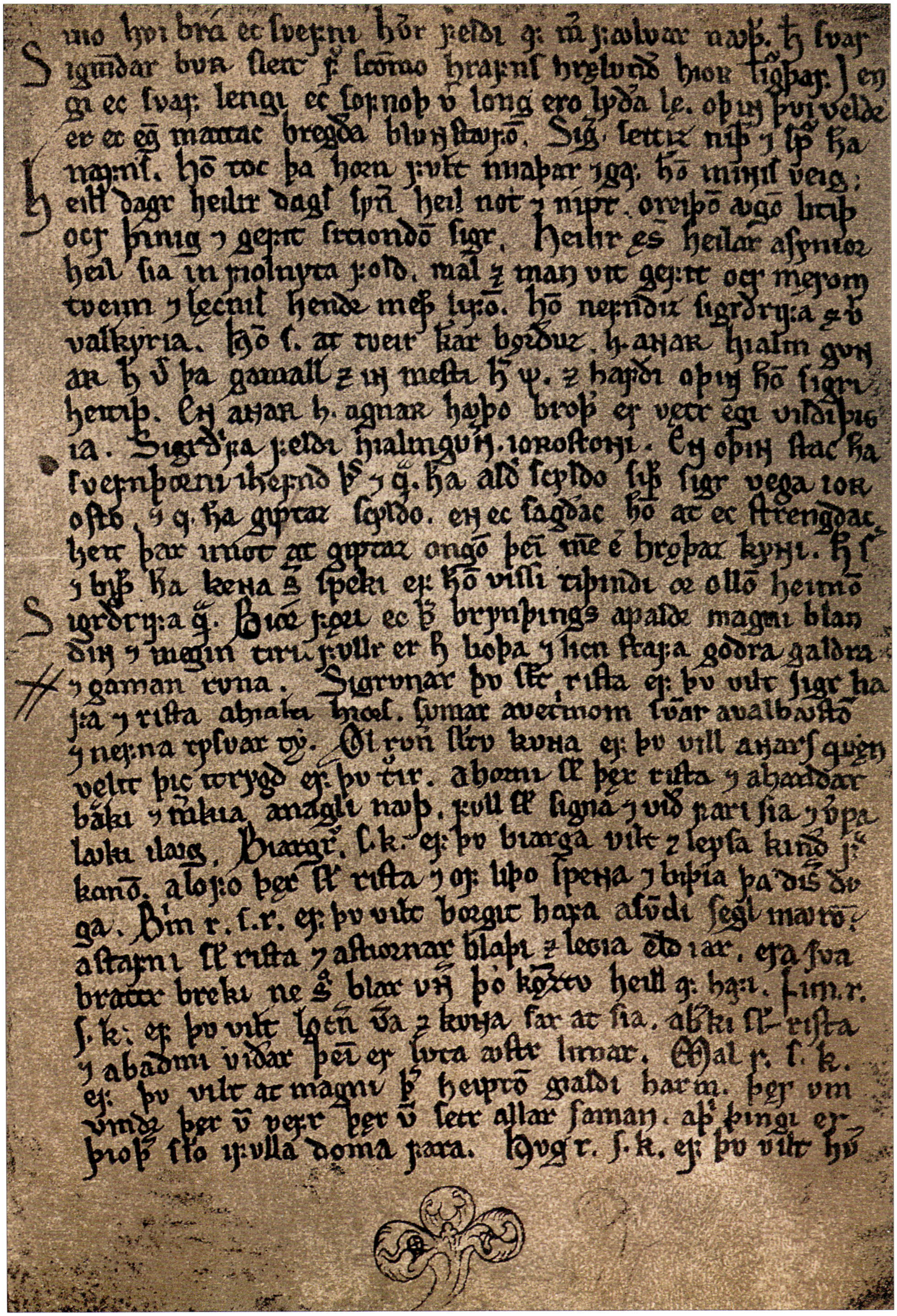

A page taken from a version of the Edda *handwritten in 1280.*

The Slaying of the Serpent Fafnir

Regin's plan was to have Sigurd kill the serpent Fafnir so that he, Regin, could finally get the gold he felt was rightfully his. But Sigurd insisted on avenging the death of his father first. Riding his magnificent horse, Grani, Sigurd set out to battle the sons of Hunding. After he killed the Hundings and got his revenge, Sigurd set off with Regin to find the terrible serpent Fafnir.

Sigurd did indeed slay the serpent with his powerful sword; afterward, when he touched a finger bloody with Fafnir's blood to his lips, he could hear the birds around him warning him about Regin's treachery. So Sigurd cut off Regin's head, ate part of Fafnir's roasted heart for courage, loaded up the cursed hoard of gold, and rode off. That is how he got the name Fafnirsbane.

The Warning

After slaying Fafnir, Sigurd rode south until he reached Mount Hindarfjall. There he met the Valkyrie Sigridrifa who read her magic runes and advised him on the future. She implored him not to seek revenge if any of his kinsmen wronged him or to let a fair woman deceive him.

Siegfried slays the terrible dragon Fafnir in the Teutonic version of the Viking myth.

The Magic of Runes

Runes were the letters of the ancient alphabet said to have been invented by the Norse god Odin. They were probably first used by Norsemen about the second or third century A.D. At first runes were simply used for scratching names on personal belongings or for marking gravestones. Later they also came to be used for divination and magic amulets. Some people were believed to have the power to "throw" a set of stones marked with rune figures and then read a person's fortune. They knew which rune figures could be best used as amulets. For example, a woman with "birth-runes" carved on the palms of her hands was a trustworthy midwife. "Wave-runes" were carved on the prows and rudders of ships to keep them safe from rough storms and high seas. "Thought-runes" carved onto shields and helmets gave their owners wisdom. A wide range of other magic runes were engraved, carved, or burned into every possible object made of stone, wood, or gold, and were shaved into the fur or cut into the hooves, tongues, beaks, and claws of every possible animal—all to give their owners special protection or powers.

78 Heroes of Scandinavian Mythology

Sigurd Falls in Love

From Mount Hindarfjall, Sigurd traveled to the Dales of Lym where he chanced to meet and fall in love with Brynhild, a Valkyrie shield maiden. He placed the ring of Andvari on her finger as a symbol of that love.

But Sigurd's travels were not over yet, and from the Dales of Lym he rode still further south until he came to the court of King Gjuki. Gjuki's sons were named Gunnar, Hogni, and Guttorm, while his daughter's name was Gudrun. Their mother, Queen Grimhild, was a scheming, ambitious woman skilled in the use of magic.

Sigurd was a very eligible bachelor and Grimhild soon decided she wanted Sigurd to marry her daughter, Gudrun. But since Sigurd was too much in love with Brynhild to even consider it, Grimhild had to resort to magic to get her way. She gave Sigurd a drink capable of stealing away a person's memory; as soon as he drank it, Sigurd forgot all about Brynhild and fell in love with Gudrun. Sigurd and Gudrun soon married. Grimhild then decided that Brynhild would be a good match for her son Gunnar and sent him off with Sigurd to bring her back.

A ring of fire burned around Brynhild's hall, and she made it known that she would only marry the man who had the courage to ride through the flames. Gunnar tried, using first his own horse, then Sigurd's horse, Grani, but failed both times. But Sigurd knew that he himself could do it, so he and Gunnar agreed that Sigurd would dress up like Gunnar, ride through the flames on Grani, and wed Brynhild in her own hall. The earth shook and the flames stretched up as far as the heavens, but he did it.

That night, before going to sleep, Sigurd (disguised as Gunnar) laid his sword between himself and Brynhild. They exchanged rings, so that Sigurd once more got possession of the ring of Andvari and gave her another ring in its place. The next day, Sigurd and Gunnar resumed their true identities. As soon as Gunnar and Brynhild were officially married, the magic potion wore off and Sigurd remembered his all-consuming love for Brynhild. But they were both married to other people now, and the noble Sigurd would say nothing that would betray his true feelings.

Stone runes were used by the Vikings for divination and as magic amulets.

80 Heroes of Scandinavian Mythology

Brynhild's Revenge

Some time later, Brynhild and Gudrun got into a fight over who had the best husband. When Gudrun asserted that no one, not even Gunnar, could compare with her hero husband, Sigurd Fafnirsbane, Brynhild pointed out that nothing could be braver than riding through the ring of fire—which was what Gunnar had done to win her hand. It was then that Gudrun laughed spitefully and said, "Do you really think it was Gunnar who rode through the fire that day? No, it was Sigurd! Afterward he took the ring of Andvari from your hand—and gave it to me!"

Brynhild grew pale with rage and grief when she finally understood what had happened, but said nothing. Sick at heart, she took to her bed and could not be consoled by anyone. Finally Sigurd came and confessed his love for her. He even promised to kill Gudrun so that he and Brynhild could run away together and be married. But Brynhild was too proud to listen. Rather than marry Sigurd on such terms, she decided she'd rather see him dead. Unwilling to do the deed himself, Gunnar got Sigurd and Gudrun's own young son, Guttorm, drunk on serpent's and wolf's blood and had him stab Sigurd in his sleep.

After calling out to her brother Atli to seek revenge after she was gone, Brynhild planned the funeral. Just before she killed herself, Brynhild's final stipulation was that her body would be burned along with Sigurd's. The magnificent funeral pyre, heaped with Sigurd's slaves and servants who had the honor of being burned along with him, shot its flames up to the very heavens.

Atli's Revenge

Gunnar and his brother Hogni inherited all of Sigurd's treasures after his death and the power of the curse continued. Atli, Brynhild's brother, claimed that the two of them had caused Brynhild's death and threatened them with war. Their scheming mother, Grimhild, however, kept the peace by brewing up another batch of her potion of forgetfulness and married Atli off to the widowed Gudrun.

But Atli had his eye on the gold, too. He invited his brothers-in-law Gunnar and Hogni to a great banquet with the secret intention of killing them and seizing the treasure. But, sensing that something was wrong, the brothers decided to hide Fafnir's gold at the bottom of the river before they left.

As the two brothers neared Atli's court, Atli's men sprang out and attacked them, and a terrible battle took place. The brothers fought bravely but in the end were captured. Atli tortured them to find where they had hidden the

below
The morning after he rode through flames to win Brynhild's hand in marriage, Sigurd (disguised as Gunnar) woke her so that they could exchange rings. Later that day, Sigurd and Gunnar resumed their true identities.

opposite
Brynhild's treacherous brother Atli tries to coerce his brother-in-law Gunnar into revealing where he hid the Nibelung's treasure.

This eighth-century stone carving shows Gudrun killing her two young sons in her gruesome plot to get even with her husband Atli.

gold, but they bravely kept their secret until they died.

Gudrun Seeks Revenge

Horrified at the death of her brothers, Gudrun then plotted her own revenge, and her plan was a gruesome one. First she killed the two small sons she had had by Atli. She made drinking vessels from their skulls and gave him wine to drink mixed with the blood of his children. She also served him their hearts at dinner. When she told him afterwards what she had done, Atli was filled with sorrow or the death of his sons—and with fear for what Gudrun might try to do next.

He was right to be afraid. That night she waited until he was asleep, then crept to his bedside and stabbed him in the breast. Afterward she set fire to his hall, killing most of his men.

82 Heroes of Scandinavian Mythology

The Ring of the Nibelungen

Almost all the Germanic cultures (Scandinavian, Icelandic, Teutonic) that existed in northern Europe had the same legends, only the names of the characters and some of the plot details varied. For example, in the old Teutonic saga *The Song of the Nibelungs* (the story that became the subject of Richard Wagner's Ring operas), the Norse characters of Sigmund and Signy are named Siegmund and Sieglinda, while Sigmund's son Sigurd and his wife Gudrun become Siegfried and Kriémhild.

In the Teutonic version of the story, the hoard of gold originally exists in the depths of the Rhine River, guarded by the innocent and beautiful Rhine maidens. But one of the Nibelungs, a dwarf named Alberich, tricks the Rhine maidens into giving him the gold, which he then fashions into a powerful magic ring. Trouble starts when the gods don't have the money to pay the giants they commissioned to build them a castle. After the gods Wotan and Loki steal the ring from Alberich to give to the giants, Alberich lays a terrible curse on the ring and all those who will ever own it.

The curse begins at once when one giant, Fafner, kills his brother to get the treasure, then turns himself into a dragon to guard his wealth. The plot follows the Volsung Saga pretty closely except that Siegfried's tutor (the character who convinces Siegfried to slay the dragon) is Mime, Alberich's scheming brother, who is plotting to double-cross Siegfried and get the gold ring for himself. After Siegfried falls in love with the ex-Valkyrie, Brünnhilde, he is tricked by Alberich's evil dwarf son, Hagen, into forgetting his love for Brünnhilde and marrying Hagen's half-sister Gutrune instead. As in the Norse version, Siegfried is killed. Out of her all-consuming love for him, Brünnhilde takes the magic ring from his finger, places it on her own, and dies riding her steed into the flames of Siegfried's funeral pyre.

The four operas that make up Wagner's Ring Cycle are *Prologue: Das Rheingold*; *Part I: Die Walkyrie*; *Part II: Siegfried*; and *Part III: Götterdämerung* or Twilight of the Gods. The ending to the Ring Cycle, *Götterdämerung*, is more dramatic than the Norse version of the myth.

Valhalla, the hall of the gods, collapses and the Rhine River overflows. Hagen the dwarf manages to snatch the gold ring from the ashes in all the confusion but is immediately pulled under and drowned for his treachery by the Rhine maidens, who then reclaim their ring treasure. The gods are destroyed, but the world has been purged by love and a new era awaits.

Hagen the evil dwarf manages to snatch the gold ring but is then drowned by the Rhine Maidens.

Heroes of Scandinavian Mythology 83

Chapter 5

Heroes of Asian Mythology

Some of the oldest cultures and mythologies in the world originated in Eastern Asia, a large area that includes Japan, Korea, China, India, and all the countries of Southeast Asia such as Cambodia and Thailand. Ancient myths about spirits, ghosts, dragons, and monstrous snakes can be traced back more than 4,000 years. Some of the old myths were very complex, with hundreds of different gods ruling in the kingdoms of Heaven and the Underworld as well as on Earth. Except in India, ancestor myths were also very widespread.

Many of the original myths changed when they came into contact with widespread religious influences such as Buddhism, Confucianism, and Hinduism, all of which have their own myths and hero legends. Other old stories simply continued to exist alongside the newer ones.

Some of the most colorful hero stories can be found in such great Hindu poems as the Mahabharata *and* Ramayana, *which depict epic battles between good and evil.*

Haemosu and the River Earl's Daughters
A Korean Tale

When the hero Haemosu, a true Son of Heaven, first came to earth one summer very long ago, his arrival was glorious: he soared down from the heavens in a five-dragon chariot followed by hundreds of robed followers all riding on swans. The mountains echoed with chiming music and banners floated on the colorfully tinted clouds. The men chosen to rule on earth had always come down from heaven, but never like this. From then on, King Haemosu lived and ruled on earth among humans during the day, but every evening he climbed into his dragon chariot and

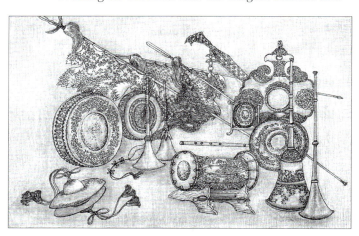

Processioners played beautifully decorated horns and drums and waved colorfully embroidered banners to announce the arrival of their celestial hero.

journeyed the hundreds of thousands of miles back to his palace in Heaven.

One day King Haemosu was out hunting near the Green River when he caught sight of the River Earl's three beautiful daughters playing among the green waves of the Bear's Heart Pool. Their jade ornaments tinkled as they splashed in the water and their modest, flowerlike beauty made them seem as delicate as fairies. The king was immediately enchanted and started toward the girls, but when the three sisters saw him coming, they plunged under the water and fled.

Obsessed with the idea of meeting them, Haemosu built a magnificent palace near the riverbank. When the three maidens came upon the seemingly deserted palace, they entered and found elegant cushions and golden goblets of wine which the king had set out for them. Delighted with their good fortune, they drank the wine and soon became a little tipsy. When the king emerged from his hiding place where he was spying on them, the startled girls ran. But the oldest, Wildflower, tripped and fell and so the king caught her.

When the River Earl heard about this, he raged in anger. He sent a speedy messenger to the king demanding an explanation. Eager to clear up the matter, Haemosu got into his dragon chariot and flew to the Ocean Palace where the River Earl lived. He explained to the River Earl that he was a true Son of Heaven, sent to earth to rule as king, and that he wanted Wildflower by his side. The River Earl admonished him, pointing out that not even kings could simply go

86 Heroes of Asian Mythology

Korean mythology includes several stories about powerful woman warriors. In this engraving, the defeated men of Shinra submit themselves to the conquering Queen Jingu.

around kidnapping the women they want to marry. Besides, how could he be sure Haemosu was really the Son of Heaven as he said he was?

To test the king's powers of transformation, the River Earl leapt into the river's rippling green waters and changed himself into a carp. The king immediately turned himself into an otter and seized the carp before it could swim away. So then the River Earl sprouted wings and transformed himself into a pheasant, but the king became a golden eagle and immediately swooped down on the pheasant with his talons.

After a number of other tests, the River Earl finally conceded that the king was, in fact, divine. He poured some of his best wine and proposed a toast to the wedding couple. But just to make sure the king really intended to marry his daughter, he got Haemosu drunk and put him in a leather bag. Then he set the bag in the dragon chariot beside Wildflower and sent the chariot off to the heavens. But before the dragons had even left the ground, Haemosu awoke from his stupor. Angrily seizing the girl's golden hairpin, he pierced the leather, slid out through the hole, and took off for the heavens—leaving his new wife behind. He did not return.

Although it was certainly not Wildflower's fault, the furious River Earl punished his daughter by having her lips stretched three feet wide and then throwing her into the river Ubal. Eventually a passing fisherman from a nearby kingdom saw the strange and frightful sight and took her home in his net to show to his ruler, King Kûmwa.

Wildflower's stretched-out lips had made her mute and the King's servants had to trim her lips three times before she could finally speak. After hearing her sad story, King Kûmwa took pity on her and offered to let her stay in his palace. Four years later, Wildflower gave birth to

Heroes of Asian Mythology 87

An intense love of their country's mountains, rivers, as well as the influences of Buddhism, Taoism, and especially Confucianism over the last several thousand years have helped form Korea's rich mythology.

a large, strangely shaped egg that frightened everyone who saw it. She named the egg Chumong. Even though he knew its father was Haemosu, King Kûmwa believed that anything born from an egg like that would be monstrous and inhuman and should therefore be destroyed. He ordered the egg put out into the horse corral, but the horses took great care not to trample it. Then the king ordered it repeatedly thrown down steep hills, but the wild beasts all protected it.

Finally, a fox retrieved the egg and gave it back to Wildflower, who carefully nurtured it until an infant boy hatched. As Chumong grew to be a strong and intelligent child, his mother told him how his father, Haemosu, had come to earth from Heaven in a dragon chariot and how Chumong himself was destined to become a great king one day when he was grown. She made him a bow and arrows and he soon became an expert marksman.

As the years passed and Chumong became an impressive warrior, King Kûmwa's sons became jealous and begged their father to do something. So the king put Chumong in charge of tending horses. Humiliated, Chumong decided he would rather die than live in such shame; he took his trusty stallion, said good-bye to his tearful mother, and made his escape. King Kûmwa, who didn't want Chumong setting up an enemy kingdom nearby, sent his warriors in hot pursuit.

Chumong traveled south until he reached the River Om, but then could find no ferry to cross it. He raised his whip to the sky and uttered a long, sad cry imploring his father to help him in his flight from danger. To his amazement, as soon as he touched the water with his bow, all the fish and turtles hurried to put their heads and tails together to form a great bridge. Chumong hurried across just as the king's troops caught up with him. When the king's men tried to set foot on the bridge, the animals all let go and it simply melted away.

Free at last, Chumong rode until he found an unspoiled land of mountains and streams and beautiful, thick-wooded hills. There, he proclaimed himself King Tongmyông. No sooner had he uttered the words than thousands upon thousands of carpenters descended from the heavens to build the new king a royal palace. Tongmyông became a great and beloved king who reigned for many years.

The King Who Was Fried
A Tale from India

A long time ago, there lived an Indian king named Karan who had made a vow never to eat breakfast until he had given away one hundred pounds in gold to the poor. Early each morning the palace servants would come out with baskets and baskets of gold pieces to scatter among the throngs of poor people crowded around the palace gate. Then, after the last piece of gold had been given away, King Karan would sit down to his breakfast and enjoy it the way he felt a man as charitable as he deserved to enjoy it.

The king's subjects worried that sooner or later the king's treasury would be used up and then everyone in the kingdom (including the king) would starve, but every day, day in and day out, for years and years, the king continued to give away one hundred pounds of gold every morning.

There was, of course, a secret to King Karan's bottomless supply of gold, which none of his servants or subjects knew about. It was quite simple: he had made a pact with the hungry old fakir (a hermit with powers of sorcery) who lived on top of the hill. Every day the fakir would conjure up one hundred pounds of gold to give to the king, on the condition that every day the king would allow himself to be fried and eaten by the fakir.

If an ordinary person had fried and eaten the king, of course, the king would have been dead the first day. But the fakir was no ordinary person. After he had eaten the king and picked his bones clean, he would simply put the bones back together, say a charm or two, and the king would suddenly be alive again, as fat and jolly as ever. While the king certainly did not find it pleasant to be sizzled in a frying pan every morning until he was crisp and brown, and then eaten, he soon got used to it and considered it a small price to pay to be able to give away gold daily to his poor subjects.

When King Karan heard the beautiful birds singing in his neighboring ruler's kingdom, he became intensely jealous and ordered his servants to kidnap them.

Heroes of Asian Mythology **89**

It also happened that around a nearby lake there lived beautiful wild swans that could only eat pearls. One day pearls had become so scarce that the swans were forced to fly throughout the land in a desperate search of more. When Bikramajit, the king of a nearby kingdom and Karan's enemy, saw the starving birds, he ordered his servants to spread pearls out for them in the courtyards. The wild swans were so grateful that they flew through the countryside singing the praises of King Bikramajit.

King Karan heard the birds singing as he breakfasted each morning, and he soon became jealous. After all, look at all the trouble he put himself through each day to be charitable and no one was singing *his* praises. King Karan ordered his servants to catch and cage the wild swans so he could give them his own pearls to eat. But the birds refused King Karan's pearls and just kept singing about how great King Bikramajit was.

When word got back to King Bikramajit that King Karan was holding the swans captive, he disguised himself as one of Karan's servants to spy on him. Guessing that there must be a secret to all the gold King Karan was giving away, King Bikramajit followed him one morning and watched as the fakir fried and ate him before sending him back down the hillside with one hundred pounds of gold.

The next morning, King Bikramajit got up at the crack of dawn and slashed himself all over with a carving knife. Then he rubbed a mixture of salt, pepper, and spices into the gashes, and when he was through climbed up the hill to the fakir's house and popped himself into the waiting frying pan. The fakir was still asleep but soon woke when he heard the sizzling.

Amazed at how appetizing King Karan smelled when he was "deviled" with such wonderful spices, the fakir gobbled up King Bikramajit, and afterward shook out his magic coat to give him the gold. Still thinking his breakfast had been King Karan, the delighted fakir implored him to show up deviled every morning, promising him anything he wanted in return. King Bikramajit asked for the old fakir's magic coat and received it.

Feeling stuffed and sleepy from his delicious breakfast, the fakir soon fell sound asleep. By the time the real King Karan showed up to be fried, the fakir was not the least bit hungry. "But it wasn't me who showed up deviled this morning," the king shouted. "At least give me the gold then since I'm still more than willing to be eaten!" "Sorry," said the fakir, "but I can't. That fine-tasting man I had for breakfast took my magic coat."

So King Karan returned home in despair and ordered his servants to take the day's gold out of the royal treasury so he could eat his breakfast in peace. By the fourth day, the royal treasury was empty and because he was a man of his word, the king stopped eating breakfast.

Days passed and King Karan became thinner and thinner. Finally, King Bikramajit took pity on the gloomy old man and showed him the magic coat he had taken from the fakir. He offered to give it to King Karan in exchange for freeing the wild swans.

When the birds were set free, they continued to sing the praises of King Bikramajit, but this time King Karan hung his head in shame. "The swans' song is true," he said. "I let myself be fried so I could give away gold every day—only so that I could eat my breakfast without feeling guilty. Bikramajit not only let himself be fried but deviled, too, and he endured all that just to free some swans!"

opposite
The king who lived in this opulent palace felt too guilty to eat breakfast each day until he had given away 100 pounds of gold pieces to the poor people who crowded around his palace gates. And to get the gold, he had to let himself be fried.

opposite
This Chinese mural painting depicts a mendicant friar in the company of a tiger. Such monks would wander the Chinese countryside relying on the generosity of strangers for their food and drink.

Flood Legends

Almost every ancient civilization has a legend about a terrible flood that covers the whole earth and destroys almost all the living plants and animals, with only a chosen few spared. Western society has the story of Noah and the Ark as recounted in Genesis, the first book of the Bible. In Greek mythology, Zeus decides to destroy the earth with a flood, and it's King Deucalion and his family who take refuge in an ark.

Eastern mythology has its own powerful flood heroes. Indian texts dating back to the sixth century B.C. tell the story of how Manu is warned by a giant fish with golden scales about the coming of a terrible seven-day deluge. The magic fish directs him to build a huge boat, then to gather up a pair of each of the earth's creatures, as well as the seeds of every plant.

The flood legends in Chinese mythology (and there are several) have a different twist. In ancient China, floods were feared because they wiped out precious crops and caused famine. In one story, the legendary hero Yü the Great not only rescues the world from devastating floodwaters, but with the help of a magic dragon and turtle, dredges gullies and valleys into the land so that future floods will have a way to recede out to the sea without washing away fields of crops.

Southern China has a flood myth called the Gourd Children in which a poor farmer hears distant thunder and fears a coming flood, so he tricks Wen Zhong, the terrible, red-haired God of Thunder, by impaling him on his hay fork and locking him in a cage. Intending to pickle him, the farmer goes off to the village to buy some herbs. Meanwhile, the Thunder God bursts out of his cage and starts a terrible deluge of rain. The farmer returns just in time to put his children into hollow gourds so they will float on top of the floodwaters. All the people on earth (including the farmer) are wiped out by the flood except for the farmer's children bobbing around in the gourds; they become known as Fu Xi, the gourd children. When the waters finally subside and the children are grown, they marry and eventually repopulate the earth.

Eyebrows Twelve Inches Apart
A Chinese Hero Legend

As in other cultures, there are many popular Chinese hero stories that fall into the category of revenge myth. The hero of this revenge story is named Ch'ih Pi (which means "eyebrows twelve inches apart") and he's the son of another legendary hero, the sword maker Kan Chiang.

Kan Chiang was a master sword crafter, perhaps the best in the kingdom of Wu. He and his wife, Mo Yeh, had only one son, a fine-looking lad whom they named Ch'ih Pi because his eyebrows were twelve inches apart.

When their son was only six, Kan Chiang sent three swords of exceptionally fine workmanship to King Ho Lü as a gift. The king was so impressed that he ordered Kan Chiang to make him two more. Kan Chiang carefully selected only the purest iron and gold from the five mountains and then waited for the perfect day on which to forge them, the day when the cosmic forces of female and male (Yin and Yang) were in perfect harmony. He waited three years.

In spite of all his best efforts, however, the molten essences of the gold and iron refused to fuse and liquefy. Kan Chiang just could not understand it, but his wife and assistant, Mo Yeh, knew that it was because the gods of metallurgy had not been properly appeased. She knew exactly what to do: she cut off her hair and fingernails and threw herself into the fire.

As Mo Yeh's body burned in the fire, the gold and iron liquefied as if by magic and the metal was transformed into two of the most wondrous of swords. Kan Chiang decorated them with turquoise stones and ornate inscriptions. He hid one of the swords under a rock up on the mountainside, and then rode off to present the other to the king.

The king loved the sword but was angry that it had taken more than three years to make. He was even more angry that there was only one sword and not the two he had requested. Kan Chiang told him that yes, he had produced two swords as ordered, but he had hidden the other in a safe place, just in case the king threatened to kill him. The king was so angry he ordered Kan Chiang killed anyway.

Kan Chiang had arranged for a trusted servant to tell his young son, Ch'ih Pi, where the sword was hidden when he was old enough to use it. Ten years later Ch'ih Pi split the rock apart

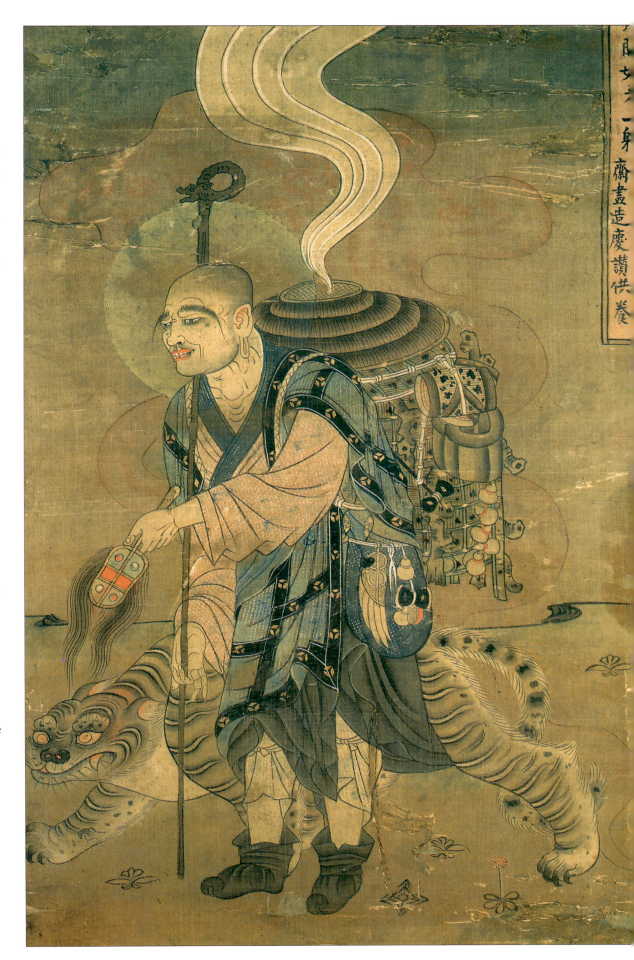

with an ax, and from the moment he saw the beautiful sword, all he could think about was killing the king to avenge his father's death.

About that same time the King started having nightmares. He dreamt he saw a young lad with eyebrows twelve inches apart trying to kill him, a boy screaming for revenge. The king was so upset that the next day he immediately offered a ransom of a thousand pieces of gold for anyone who brought him the boy answering this description. When Ch'ih Pi heard of this, he fled to the forest in despair.

One day a stranger met him in the woods and asked him why he was so sad. Ch'ih Pi explained how the king had killed his father and now it was practically impossible for him to get revenge. "Well," said the stranger, "the king is offering a ransom of a thousand pieces of gold for your head, right? I could get in to see him—and get your revenge for you—if I could bring him your head and your sword."

"That is a very good idea," said Ch'ih Pi, who promptly slit his own throat and handed his head and sword to the stranger. Before Ch'ih Pi's headless corpse toppled over, the startled stranger said, "I will not fail you!"

The king's servants boiled the head of Ch'ih Pi in a fandang, *an immense, rectangular cooking vessel made of bronze and traditionally decorated with human faces.*

When the stranger showed up with the boy's head, the king was overjoyed. The stranger told him that since it was the head of a very brave man, it should be boiled in a large pot. The king agreed and had his servants get a cauldron ready. Though the servants boiled the head for three days and three nights, it would not cook through. Ch'ih Pi's head just kept bobbing angrily on top of the water, its blazing eyes flashing with rage. Finally, the stranger suggested that maybe if the king looked at it himself the head would be more likely to cook properly.

The king got up at once and approached the cauldron. As soon as he reached it, the stranger crept up behind him and lopped off his head with the boy's sword, toppling it into the boiling water. Then the stranger lopped off his own head, and still another head fell into the cauldron. The three heads now cooked quickly, and by the time the flesh finally fell from the skulls, it was impossible to tell anymore who was who. The servants took the pile of flesh and buried it up on the mountainside. They named the site the Grave of the Three Kings.

The Monkey King
A Chinese Adventure Story

The Monkey King is a renowned classical Chinese novel that dates back over four hundred years. It's a book with everything: an amazing plot filled with adventure and mingled with an assortment of Chinese fables, fairy tales, legends, superstitions, monster stories, and battles.

According to legend, Monkey was a rebellious and most extraordinary human being. Born out of a rock and fertilized by the grace of Heaven, he was extremely smart and capable even as a child. He was raised by a master Taoist who carefully taught him all he knew about magic and kung fu, so that by the time he was a young man, he had the ability to transform himself into seventy-two different images—everything from a tree to a mosquito to a beast of prey. Monkey learned to travel by using clouds, but could also easily cover thousands and thousands of miles in a single graceful somersault.

Monkey became even more rebellious as he got older, despising feudal authority and claiming that there was no higher authority than his own, anywhere. That included not just the earth but the heavens, the seas, and the subterranean world of hell as well. The rulers of these realms did not appreciate Monkey's treasonous attitude and sent their massive armies to fight him.

After many showdowns, the armies of Heaven finally persuaded the emperor of the earthly kingdom to offer Monkey an official title to appease him. Monkey accepted the offer on a trial basis. However, when he learned a few days later that the position he was given was actually nothing more than the emperor's stable keeper, he was outraged. He had been cheated and he knew that everyone on earth and in Heaven was laughing at him for it. Enraged, he declared himself Supreme King and immediately declared war on everyone in the universe.

It was a long fight and it took the help of all the warrior-gods in heaven, but eventually the Monkey King was defeated. The plan was to execute him, but every method of execution they tried failed. They couldn't even behead him because he turned his head into bronze and his shoulders into iron. Finally, as a last resort, the emperor commanded that the Monkey King be burned in the same furnace where the emperor's ministers were working on refining his immortality pills. But instead of killing him, the white-hot fire and choking smoke only crystallized the Monkey King's eyes into golden fire crystals, giving him extraordinary powers of sight. With the help of his new vision, Monkey escaped.

Finally, when all else failed to stop the Monkey King, the armies of Heaven and earth called upon the Buddha for help. The Buddha caused the great mountain known as the Mount of Five Fingers to fall upon him, yet the tenacious Monkey somehow miraculously survived the enormous weight and pressure. He was alive and saw through things ordinary people

The monkey has symbolized many different things in Chinese culture, from trickster to Buddhist god.

Heroes of Asian Mythology 95

couldn't—but he wasn't able to move for about five hundred years!

Finally, a Tang monk named Xuan Zang came along and rescued him. In gratitude, Monkey agreed to become his disciple and to escort him on his holy journey west. And that is the start of a whole new chapter of the Monkey King's adventures: he befriends an over-the-hill sea monster and a grumpy pig that was once a high-ranking general, until he is punished for assaulting a fairy.

A Japanese demon mask from a thirteenth-century Noh drama.

No Place to Hide!

The heroes of Japanese myths and legends had to battle some of the weirdest and most terrifying monsters in world mythology. Here are just a few examples:

Oni—An Oni is a huge, fanged ogre with the muscles and horns of a bull. His tough skin can be red, blue, or black and he has the ability to reconnect and heal severed limbs instantly. Most live in Jigoku (Hell), although many prefer to live on earth, usually disguised as beautiful women. Oni are considered to be highly intelligent and extremely difficult to kill. They also have a passion for eating human flesh.

Tengu—The tengu are supernatural creatures with the bodies of humans and the spirits of mountains. A Tengu usually looks like a tall, thin man with a very large nose and a red face, although some are small and have the head and wings of a black crow. A Tengu is usually seen wearing a pair of *geta* (Japanese wooden sandals) and carrying a magic fan made of bird feathers with which to create terrible tornadoes. Although they have no wings, Tengu have the ability to fly. Their main function is to keep human society in chaos by provoking war and civil disorder.

Kappa—Every river is inhabited by at least one Kappa, an evil dwarf with green, scaled skin, dangerous razor-sharp sickles for appendages, and a hollow in the top of a flat head to hold poisonous water. A Kappa's idea of fun is to gash a person's abdomen and then steal his or her *shirokodama* (bowels). But their all-consuming passion is eating cucumbers, which is why cucumber sushi is called "Kappa-maki."

Henge—The Henge are certain foxes, raccoons, and other wild animals who have the ability to transform themselves into human beings and to create other illusions. Living mostly in the mountains, they take particular delight in tricking hunters and woodsmen. (They can make leaves look like money bills, for example, or horse excrement look like roast beef.) Henges often try to divert heroes

The wild and hideous Henge delight in tricking hunters and woodsman with their ability to transform themselves into humans and to create other illusions.

from their quests by turning themselves into beautiful and seductive women.

Gaki—The Gaki are ghastly, thin, undead creatures from *Jigoku* (Hell) who are condemned to wander for eternity suffering endless hunger and thirst. In their desperate need to satisfy their appetites, these ghoulish monsters will eat anything, but prefer human flesh and blood.

Nurikabe—A Nurikabe is a huge invisible wall with arms and legs that allow it to move around the countryside and block roadways. Nurikabes can be very frustrating to heroes in a hurry.

Ittan-momen—An Ittan-momen is a nasty little creature that looks like a simple white cloth flapping in the breeze. Appearing suddenly in the night, it suffocates its victim by wrapping itself around the person's mouth and nose.

Minamoto-no-Yorimitsu and the Evil Oni
A Japanese Hero Legend

A thousand years ago a terrible oni by the name of Shuten Doji was terrorizing Kyoto. He looked like a huge, hideously disfigured blue ox with leering fangs, and lived in his own palace high atop a nearby mountain. He hadn't always been an oni. Once he had been a human robber, but because he had killed so many people, he was made to look like the monster he really was.

The emperor called upon the kingdom's most respected sword master, Minamoto-no-

Yorimitsu, to track down and slay the hideous monster. Yorimitsu took four of his best men and headed for the oni's castle on Mount Oe. The men disguised themselves as mountain hermits, and as they climbed up the mountain, they met three mysterious old men who gave Yorimitsu a magic helmet and a bottle of magical wine called Shinbenkidokushu.

When they reached the castle of Shuten Doji on Mount Oe, Doji looked at their hermit clothing, then invited them in and asked them to stay for dinner. Although the oni seemed quite friendly and hospitable, Yorimitsu knew the banquet was really a test; when Doji served them human flesh, they ate every morsel so their host would believe their false identities. The ruse

The emperor called on Minamoto-no-Yorimitsu to stop the hideous oni Shuten Doji from terrorizing the Japanese kingdom of Kyoto, depicted on this seventeenth-century screen.

worked. When they offered to share their wine with their generous host and poured him a cup of the magic Shinbenkidokushu, the thirsty Doji drank it down in a single gulp.

The wine did in fact make Doji very sleepy, but even though it was five against one and even though the monster was practically unconscious, it was still a long and bloody battle. Over and over again, Yorimitsu and his four great swordsmen assaulted Doji, sticking their spears through his body and cutting at his head, but Doji resisted violently. Finally, with a tremendous swipe, Yorimitsu cut off the oni's head. But before the oni died, his disembodied head jumped up and tried to take a bite out of *Yorimitsu's* head with his enormous jaws. If Yorimitsu had not been

Heroes of Asian Mythology 99

wearing the magic helmet the old men had given him, he would have been killed instantly. With a great shudder, the oni Shuten Doji finally died. When they brought his head back to the emperor as proof, Minamoto-no-Yorimitsu was proclaimed a great hero throughout the land.

Izanagi and Izanami
A Tragic Japanese Love Story

Many, if not most, of the heroes of Asian mythology are gods and goddesses whose heroic feats were responsible for creating all the phenomena of the universe. Often they take on very human characteristics and emotions when dealing with each other, as in this story of the hero Izanagi's attempt to rescue his beloved Izanami.

Izanagi and Izanami were the first male and female deities brought forth by the gods. Their job was to form the oceans, mountains, and islands of the earth and to give birth to all the other deities which would rule them. Joined together as husband and wife, the two created the earth by throwing their spears into the muddy chaos of the universe from a celestial bridge. Then they descended to the earth and Izanami gave birth to the islands and continents.

Izanami had already given birth to a number of deities (including Ohowatatsumi, the God of the Sea, Shimatsuhiko, the God of the Wind, and Kukunoshi, the God of the Mountains) when she became so burned giving birth to the God of Fire that she died. Sick with despair, her husband Izanagi cried over her, and from the tears that dropped onto her pillow sprang still other divinities into existence. Izanagi was so enraged by his wife's death that he took his sword and cut off his newborn son's head, and from the blood that spurted all over the room, still more deities were born.

Izanami descended to the Land of Darkness, the underworld of the dead, where she built a castle for herself. Izanagi, who could not bear the thought of living without her, implored her to return, but she hesitated, saying it was too late because she had already tasted the food of the Land of Darkness. Finally, Izanami went to ask the gods of the Land of Darkness if they could

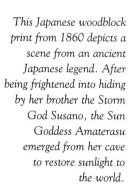

This Japanese woodblock print from 1860 depicts a scene from an ancient Japanese legend. After being frightened into hiding by her brother the Storm God Susano, the Sun Goddess Amaterasu emerged from her cave to restore sunlight to the world.

100 Heroes of Asian Mythology

make an exception in her case and let her return to earth. They said yes, on the condition that her husband would promise to wait for her without trying to see her.

Izanagi agreed, but the waiting was long and he soon grew impatient. One day he broke off the left tooth of his comb, set it on fire so he could see where he was going, and entered the Land of Darkness to look for Izanami and find out what was taking her so long. He finally found Izanami, but the sight of her was shocking and horrible. Her badly decomposing, maggot-ridden corpse was lying on the ground guarded by the Eight Thunders.

Angry and humiliated to be seen in such a shameful state, Izanami sent the horrible *Shikome* (the Ugly Females of the Land of Darkness) after her husband. Izanagi managed to outwit them as he fled, by taking his headdress off and throwing it behind him; it immediately turned into grapes which the old hags stopped to devour. Izanami then sent an army of fifteen hundred warriors after her husband. They almost captured him, but just as he reached the Even Pass, the place where the world of light meets the Land of Darkness, he found three magic peaches with which to pelt his pursuers and so he managed to escape.

Feeling defiled by his visit to this impure and disgusting place, Izanagi immediately purified himself in the waters of the river Woto. As he plunged into the water, he created the God of the Deep Sea, and as he bathed he created still more deities. Washing his nose, he gave birth to the god Takehayasusanowo; washing his right eye, he created the Goddess of the Moon, Tsukiyomi; and when he washed his left eye, he produced Amaterasu, the Goddess of the Sun.

Heroes and Creation Myths

In addition to ancestor tales of ancient rulers and stories about magic, ghosts, and other supernatural phenomena, many of the old myths in East Asia concerned themselves with creation stories.

One Chinese creation myth tells how the universe was created out of an egg that existed in total emptiness. Inside the egg was Chaos and the first god, Pangu. When the egg broke, the universe burst out and was immediately split into two parts: the heavens (yang) and the Earth (yin). This principle of opposites—yin and yang, male and female, darkness and light—continues to play an important part in Chinese Taoist philosophy and religious practice.

In the 700s A.D., Japanese scribes recorded the first written compilation of thousands of years of oral Japanese mythology. Called the *Kojiki* ("Records of Ancient Matters"), the book told how the world's first couple, Izanagi and Izanami, helped create the world.

Similar themes can be found in ancient myths throughout Southeast Asia. There are many stories that tell about fantastic animal beasts like the World Serpent Antaboga who created the World Turtle, the Underworld, and other aspects of the universe. For centuries, most of the people in these countries have lived in small communities, making their living from growing rice. As a result, myths about gods, goddesses, and heroes who can insure a good rice harvest are also common. Many other stories tell about heroic ancestors whose spirits return to protect the living from evil.

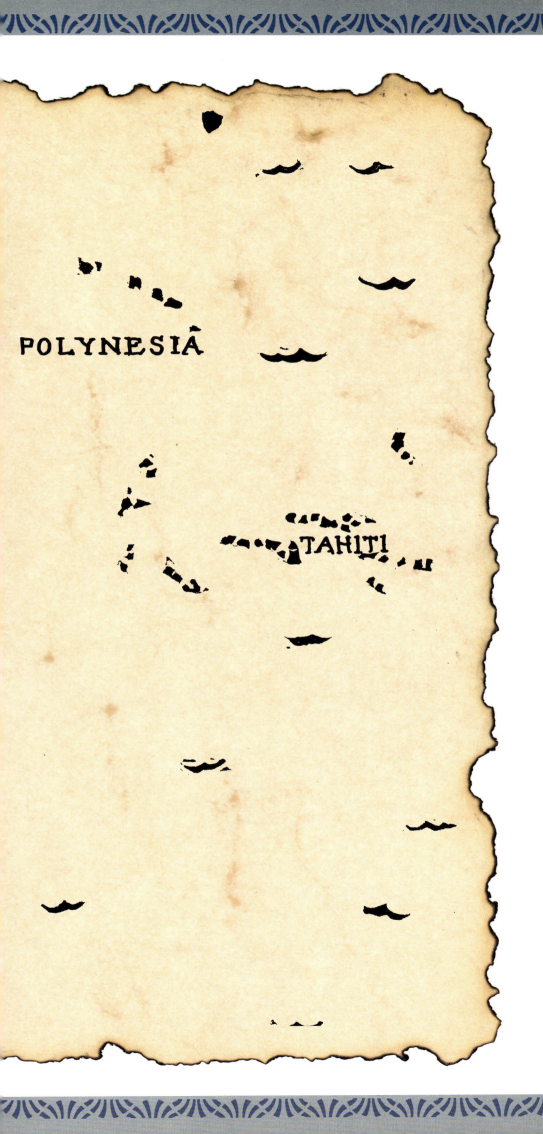

Chapter 6

Heroes of Oceanic and Australian Mythology

The South Sea Islands of Oceania are divided into three areas—Melanesia, Micronesia, and Polynesia. Each geographical area has its own mythological traditions, although all have myths that are centered around a seafaring way of life. All also tell stories about how ancestors made the sea journey from Southeast Asia to populate the islands of the South Pacific. (Anthropologists believe this migration occurred approximately 50,000 years B.C.)

Australia, which is a separate continent and therefore not considered part of Oceania (even though it is in the South Pacific), has its own distinct myths and legends. Unlike the islands of Oceania, Australia's native population is not descended from people who migrated from Southeast Asia but from the Aborigines who have lived in Australia for at least the last 50,000 years. Their myths and legends concern a "Dreamtime" when the spirits that sleep beneath the ground rose and traveled about, shaping the landscape, making people, and teaching the arts of survival. Many of their heroic ancestors were women, such as the Wawalak Sisters who fought the Great Rainbow Serpent.

6

How Maui Made the Sun Slow Down
A Maori Trickster Legend from Polynesia

One of the best-known cultural heroes in all of Oceania is the Polynesian trickster Maui. Not only is he famous for slaying monsters, rescuing maidens, defeating rivals like Tuna the Eel, and recovering his wife from the eight-eyed Bat, but also for constantly challenging the authority of the gods in order to better things for humankind.

In the hundreds of stories that have been handed down about him, Maui is portrayed as a rebel and seducer, someone who is always thumbing his nose at society's strict rules and taboos. It was through Maui's actions (sometimes inadvertent) that the world came to be as it is today. He stole the secret of fire for humans from the goddess Mahuika, fire-keeper of the underworld, by tricking her into giving him her burning fingernails. He created all of the world's islands by pulling them out of the sea with fishhooks. But in spite of all his noble and courageous deeds, Maui was still a prankster, one with a definite mean streak in him. After all, they say it was Maui who decided to permanently transform his brother-in-law into a dog just for the fun of it.

In one of the most-told stories in Polynesia, some women brought it to Maui's attention that the sun traveled so quickly that the days were too short to cook anything. No sooner did they heat their cooking stones than the sun went down and their families had to eat their half-cooked food in the dark.

Actually Maui didn't think it was a particularly challenging problem. As he told his brothers, all they had to do was make a giant noose and snare the sun with it. Then they would make it move more slowly. His brothers scoffed at him, saying the sun was far too hot and fierce to try something so ridiculous. Maui reminded them of all the wonderful and amazing things he had already accomplished—feats other people had called impossible. Besides, he said, this time he had their dead grandmother's enchanted jawbone, which he had recently acquired.

In the end, his brothers were persuaded by his arguments and agreed to help him. First they all went out collecting flax, then spent many long days spinning, twisting, and plaiting it into very stout ropes. When they had made all the ropes they needed, they stocked up on provisions and set off on their journey. They were careful to travel only by night so the sun wouldn't see them and become suspicious. At the first light of dawn each morning, they hid themselves in the forest and slept, then resumed their journey in the evening after the sun had set.

Buildings like this Maori food storehouse near the village of Rotrua, New Zealand, were often decorated with carved illustrations of trickster heroes.

They traveled eastward this way for a great long time until they finally came to the edge of the enormous pit from which the sun rose each day. Here they built a long, high wall out of clay, with huts at each end to hide in. When the wall was finished, the brothers gathered together the ropes they had made and used them to fashion a huge noose, which they tied as securely as they possibly could and placed around the rim of the pit. As they huddled in one of the huts waiting for dawn to break, Maui sat with the jawbone of their grandmother in his hand and gave his brothers their final instructions.

They were to remain hidden until the sun had risen just far enough so that his head and shoulders were through the noose. Then, when Maui shouted, they were to pull on the ropes as hard as they could and not let go for even a moment. At that point, Maui was going to jump up and knock the sun on the head with the jawbone until he was nearly (but not quite) dead. Only then would they let him loose. Whatever you do, Maui cautioned his brothers, don't be silly and start feeling sorry for him when he screams.

Finally the day dawned. The sun came up from his pit as usual, flaming red and suspecting nothing. The mountains to the west looked like they were on fire with his light. When the sun had risen far enough out of his pit so that his head and shoulders were through the noose, Maui gave the cry and his brothers pulled the noose tight. Everything went according to plan. No matter how hard the huge creature thrashed and struggled, the brothers held the ropes tight. Then Maui rushed at the sun with the enchanted jawbone and beat him so savagely about the face and head that the sun screamed and shrieked in agony.

Finally, when he knew the sun had had enough, Maui gave the signal for his brothers to let go of the rope. Once freed, the sun resumed his usual daily course, but crept slowly and feebly because of the severe pain of his wounds. And that is exactly why the sun has crept so slowly across the sky each day ever since. Thanks to Maui and his brothers, people now have time to cook their meals and to eat them while it is still daylight.

Aboriginal dance groups at Corroboree Mandora and other villages in Australia still act out myths and legends from the Dreamtime.

Dreamtime

For the aboriginal peoples of Australia, the earth was once formless and flat. Then came the Dreamtime, the period when the world was formed and all things were named. Some believe the earth's lagoons, gorges, mountains, and rivers were formed when the Giant Rainbow Serpent, Yurlunggur, wriggled and slithered across the land. During the Dreamtime, the aboriginals' ancestors traveled across the Australian landscape naming all the different land and water formations and depositing the spirits of unborn children throughout the land.

But Dreamtime (also known as Ungud or the Dreaming) is more than just a distant period of time; for many it is also a state of being. While there is a definite difference between the present, the past within a person's memory, and the distant Dreamtime past of one's ancestors, for many believers the edges of these periods can often become blurred. For example, participants in certain important rituals can enter a trance-like state in which they *become*, briefly, the wandering ancestors who originally made the legendary Dreamtime journeys. It is said that shamans have the power to slip in and out of Dreamtime to draw on knowledge for healing. Many dying people seem to slip into the Dreamtime before their deaths.

The Seven Wawalak Sisters and the Big Flood
A Yolngu tale from Northeastern Australia

The Yolngu believe that it was Yurlunggur, the Giant Rainbow Serpent, who caused the great flood during the Dreamtime. It all started when the seven Wawalak sisters set out from somewhere in the distant interior of the continent on a long and hazardous journey to the northern coast. The youngest sister was pregnant, while the oldest had a small child she carried in a paper bark cradle under her arm.

As they traveled, legend has it, the sisters hunted lizard, possum, and bandicoot and gathered plants to eat. As they walked through places, they gave names to all the plants and animals as well as to the lakes and streams and land formations—the names these things and beings still have today. One day, when the youngest sister was ready to give birth, the other sisters searched for a water hole and then collected soft bark to make her a comfortable bed. What they did not know was that the water hole they had found was inhabited by Yurlunggur, a huge, semi-human rainbow-colored serpent.

After the baby was born, one of the sisters accidentally allowed some blood to fall into the water hole when she bathed the infant. Yurlunggur rose up out of the water hole in such a rage that the water erupted and flooded the countryside. Then rain began to fall and the flood worsened.

The terrified sisters began singing songs in an attempt to stop the rain and drive the snake

Aboriginal myths tell how Australia's magnificent mountains, gorges, lagoons, and rivers were formed by the Giant Rainbow Serpent, Yurlunggur.

Heroes of Oceanic and Australian Mythology 107

away, but as they slowly tired, Yurlunggur inched his way toward them. When they finally became so exhausted that they fell asleep, Yurlunggur instantly pounced on them and swallowed them all up whole.

Now it happened that all the serpents in the land had a daily ritual that they shared, even though they all spoke different languages. They would all raise themselves up to the sky and tell each other what they had eaten that day. When it came to Yurlunggur's turn, he was so ashamed that at first he refused to say anything. But at last he admitted to having eaten the seven sisters and their children.

No sooner had he said the words than he fell to the ground in agony and spewed them back out. Although the sisters and their children were stone dead by that time, the green ants who rushed to bite them managed to revive them. As soon as they were conscious, however, Yurlunggur swallowed them up again. Then, again mortified at what he had done, the snake immediately regurgitated them again. This went on for quite a while until at last the serpent became too exhausted to continue. The floodwaters subsided and the seven Wawalak sisters and their children hurried away, grateful that they could continue their journey.

More Flood Myths

The Australian story of the Wawalak sisters is only one of the many flood tales in Oceanic mythology. In the Lake Tyres region of Australia, people tell how once all the world's water was trapped inside a giant frog and all living things were dying of thirst. The hero Eel got the frog to release the water by making silly faces at him until he laughed, but it caused a terrible flood in the process.

The legends of the Tiwi people off Australia's northern coast tell how their islands became separated from the mainland during a strange sort of Dreamtime flood when a blind old woman called Mudungkala emerged from the ground carrying three infant children—the first people on earth. As she crawled across the featureless landscape, water bubbled up in her tracks and caused a flood that permanently cut off the islands from the Australian mainland.

On the Palau Islands it is said that before humans existed, one of the Kalith gods visited an unfriendly village and was killed by its inhabitants. When his worried friends went searching for him, all the villagers were hostile and rude except for a young woman named Milathk, who told them how their friend had been murdered. The Kalith gods got their revenge by flooding the village, but only after they warned Milathk to save herself on a raft. According to the legend, it was Milathk who went on to become the mother of humankind.

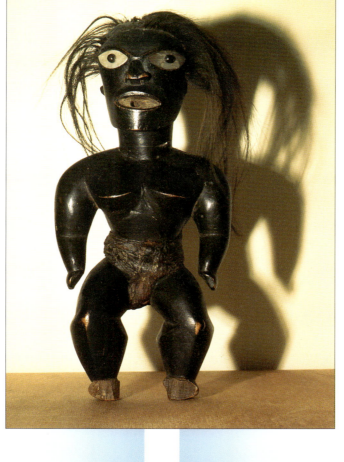

In Tahiti, legends talk about a flood so terrible that it covered the whole earth except for the very tops of the highest mountains. The flood was caused by a sea god who became enraged when his hair became entangled with the hooks a fisherman had lowered too far into the water.

A Samoan myth tells the story still another way. After the primeval octopus Hit gave birth to Fire and Water, the two children got into a terrible fight. Their splashing and thrashing about caused a terrible flood that destroyed the world, and it was then up to the god Tangaloa to re-create it.

In the islands of the New Hebrides, the story goes that Tilik and Tarai, who lived near a sacred spring where they were busy forming mountains and riverbanks, discovered to their horror that their evil mother had been urinating in their food. They exchanged the food and ate hers. When she discovered what they had done, she was so angry that she rolled away the boulder she had been using to hold back the sea. The waters immediately poured out over the land in a great and terrible flood.

left
Trickster heroes were often called upon to fight evil spirits like the Hawaiian fire goddess Pele, represented by this figurine, who lived in the crater of the Kilauea volcano.

opposite
The Maori of the Marquesas Islands and other areas of Polynesia believed in a pantheon of gods headed by the two creator beings, Rangi, the male sky, and Papa, the female earth. They also told stories of many human heroes such as Tawhaki and Rata.

Heroes of Oceanic and Australian Mythology 109

Kae and the Whale
A Hiva Oa tale from the Marquesas Islands

opposite
Hero myths of Polynesia such as the Marquesan tale of Kae and the Whale almost all centered around a seafaring way of life.

above
The spirits of ancestor heroes were considered powerful forces in the Solomon Islands. Warriors carved their images, such as this one, onto the prows of war canoes to help keep their boats on course and to ensure successful raids.

There was once an island of women called Vainoi on which there were no men at all. The women who lived there did have husbands, however, and did give birth to children. But their husbands were simply pandanus roots that they visited once in a while out in the fields.

One day, while on a sea journey, the trickster hero Kae's ship was wrecked, and he was cast ashore on this unknown island not far from the women's daily bathing spot. Kae hid himself in some bushes and spied on them until he finally realized that he was the only man on the whole island. Delighted, he came out to introduce himself to Hina, who was the island's chieftess. Hina was quite delighted herself about his being there, and the two of them were soon married.

After a while, however, Kae started to feel depressed. Part of the reason was homesickness, but the main reason was his discovery that while he grew older every day, his wife, who had supernatural powers, could regain her youth any time she wanted to just by surfing. Every month or so, all she had to do was head down to the beach and ride the waves three times in a row. On the third time, she would be carried onto the beach "as fresh as a shrimp with the shell removed." One day Hina noticed that Kae's hair was getting a little gray and suggested he come surfing with her: all Kae got from surfing were sore muscles and a bump on the head.

After a while, Hina became pregnant and gave birth to their son, but Kae continued to feel discontented. He insisted that he return to his own island for a visit to prepare certain important ceremonies for their new son. Hina knew in her heart that he would never return, but she eventually gave in and let him go. She even loaned him the use of her brother Tunua-nui, the whale, for him to ride to speed him on his journey. Before Kae left, Hina very carefully explained to him that once he reached his own island, it was very important that he turn the whale around and point him back toward the island of Vainoi.

Kae was so happy when he arrived back on his own island that he didn't bother to follow Hina's instructions. As soon as his people saw the poor animal waiting in the bay, they killed and ate him.

While Kae was busy building a house for his new son back on his own island, the boy, who was still living on Vainoi with his mother, was being tormented by his playmates for having a strange father. The boy was so miserable that, although his mother was still angry and outraged that Kae had allowed her brother to be killed and eaten, she finally agreed to let her son go to his father's island and live there with him. She put her son on the back of another great whale and gave him the same instructions she had given Kae about turning the animal around once he had reached port.

The obedient boy did as he was told, but when the greedy people on his father's island saw the whale, they rushed out to grab his tail and pull him in so they could kill and eat him like they had killed and eaten the first one. This

110 Heroes of Oceanic and Australian Mythology

time, though, it was the whale who pulled all of *them* out into deeper water where they drowned.

Meanwhile, the boy climbed up the hill looking for the house his father had built for him. When he found it, he happily bathed in the pool, ate the bananas that had been planted for him, and waited for his father. But none of the neighbors recognized him and, thinking he was a scoundrel out to steal from Kae's property, they came after him with large sticks. They would have killed him, too, if he had not shouted out his father's name at the last minute and babbled on and on about his father being the first man to ever live on the island of women. When Kae heard the boy, he ran to his side and hugged him fiercely. The next day, a great feast was held throughout Kae's land in his new son's honor.

Captain Cook collected mythological artifacts on his three voyages to the South Seas. This sculpture of the Hawaiian war god Kukailimoku has red feathers for hair, mother of pearl eyes, and real dog's teeth.

Qat, Marawa and the Sky Maiden
A tale from Banks Island and the New Hebrides

There are a number of legends in Oceanic mythology about bands of brothers. One of the brothers in a typical band (usually either the oldest or the youngest) is a hero who spends his time trying to do noble, creative deeds. The other brothers invariably give him a hard time, either through mischief, stupidity, jealousy, or greed. The most famous of these bands of brothers is the Tangaro clan: the hero Qat and his eleven brothers.

It is said that Qat and his siblings came into existence in an unusual way: on the island of Vanua Lava their mother, a large rock, sud-

denly burst into small pieces, which became her sons. Using tree stumps for canoes, Qat became a great seafarer and frequently went off on long journeys during which he created the seasons and the tides; he used fishhooks to pull new islands out of the sea. On his return Qat set out to create the island's mountains and rivers, then its trees and pigs and, finally, humans. When his brothers were tired of the constant daylight, he created the night and taught his brothers how to sleep.

In addition to having so many brothers, Qat also had an almost constant companion named Marawa, who took the shape of a spider whenever it suited him. Marawa was a bit of a trickster and was not all that smart. Although Marawa's practical jokes often exasperated Qat, Marawa had, after all, come to his rescue when Qat's wicked brothers had tried to crush him in a land-crab's hole. And when Qat was trapped in the "stretching tree," Marawa extended his long white hair as a ladder so Qat could climb down and escape.

Marawa could be good-hearted, but if it hadn't been for his foolishness, humans today

112 Heroes of Oceanic and Australian Mythology

would be as immortal as the gods. When Qat created human beings, he did it by carving the bodies of three men and three women from a tree and decorating them with swatches of palm fronds. Then he carefully hid them for three days in the shade of a clump of trees. On the fourth day, he brought the figures to life by dancing and beating a drum in front of them.

As Marawa watched Qat start to carve the figures, he wanted to make some people, too, and began to imitate him. When Qat carved, Marawa carved; when Qat hid his figures in the shade for three days, so did Marawa. But on the fourth day, when the six figures began to move in response to Qat's singing and dancing, Marawa snatched them up and ran away. He quickly dug a deep hole in the forest floor and buried them under a pile of leaves and branches. After seven days, when he reluctantly dug them back out again, the figures were lifeless, rotting bodies. Because of what Marawa did, it is said, humans can never be immortal. They are condemned to live for only a brief time on earth and then to die. Qat may have given them life, but Marawa gave them death.

According to one of the legends about Qat, it was love that finally did him in. Like the rest of his brothers, Qat acquired his wife by stealing her. One day he came upon a group of sky maidens who were bathing in a stream. While they were splashing around in the water, he crept down to the riverbank where they had laid their belongings and buried a pair of wings so one of the girls would have to stay behind when the others left. It worked, and since the poor girl had nowhere to go without her wings, she finally agreed to marry Qat.

After they were married, however, the girl became terribly sad and homesick. One day she went down to the bathing spot where she had last seen her sisters and friends. As she sat on the riverbank, she cried so hard that her tears washed away the earth that Qat had used to bury her wings. Overjoyed, she put her wings back on and flew away.

When Qat realized that his wife had left him, he became determined to find her and bring her back. First, he attached a thick rope to the end of a large, sturdy arrow, then shot the arrow up into the heavens. A long banyan root immediately appeared and wound its way down along the rope, making it easy for him to get a foothold. Qat quickly climbed up the rope into the sky world where he met a giant farmer hoeing his garden. Remembering the handy banyan root that climbed down his rope, Qat begged the man not to disturb the root until he was safely down on earth again.

Qat searched and searched the sky world until he found his estranged wife. He threw her over his shoulder and had just started climbing down the rope with her when the banyan root snapped and the rope unraveled. He let go of the girl as he fell and she quickly flew away, back up to her home in the sky world. Qat, however, could not fly, and plunged to his death.

Unlike those of Polynesia and Micronesia, Melanesian myths rarely told how the world and humanity were created by primal gods. Instead, people on Melanesian islands such as the New Hebrides believed that the landscape and original conditions for their seafaring society were established by ancestral cultural heroes like Sida, who wandered the earth.

The Exploits of Olifat
Trickster Hero of Micronesia

His name may vary a bit from island to island (some call him Iolofath or Orofad or Wolphat), but the character Olifat is well known throughout Micronesia as a notorious and often mean-spirited trickster. Although he brought many skills and benefits to humans, he also liked to make fools out of them, and many of his practical jokes caused serious injury and even death.

Olifat was like this from the moment he was born. He came into being when his father, the sky god Lugeiläng, flew down to earth to marry a mortal woman he had fallen in love with. But Lugeiläng already had a wife in the sky world, and when she found out what he was up to, she was so angry that she followed him to earth to try and stop the marriage.

It turned out that the woman Lugeiläng wanted to marry was really only *half* mortal; her mother was Hit, the primeval octopus. Hit liked Lugeiläng and approved of his marrying her daughter; each time his first wife showed up, Hit started to perform an erotic dance. This so mortified Lugeiläng's first wife that the third time she saw it, she died of embarrassment, and her attendants had to carry her dead body back up to heaven.

Lugeiläng and Hit's daughter got married as planned, but when the woman became pregnant, Lugeiläng began to feel tired of his new marriage and returned to his home in the sky. Before he left, however, he cautioned his wife never to allow their child to drink milk from a coconut through a small hole.

Like many other heroes and tricksters, Olifat had a strange birth. When the time came, his mother simply pulled on the end of a coconut leaf that she had twisted into her hair and the infant sprang out of her head. The child could run as soon as he was born.

114 Heroes of Oceanic and Australian Mythology

Olifat ate a great deal and grew very quickly. One day, when his mother wasn't watching, Olifat was thirsty. After experimenting for a while, he figured out how to punch a small hole into a coconut to get to the milk. As soon as he had his head tipped back far enough to drain the last drop, his eyes looked up at the heavens and he caught sight of his father. In spite of his mother's protests, Olifat immediately wanted to visit him. When he made up his mind, there was no stopping him. Without even saying good-bye, he scrambled up to heaven on a column of

The Gilbert Islands and other areas of Micronesia have vivid creation myths that tell how the islands, the salty sea, and the heavens were created when a caterpillar died trying to pry open a primordial clam.

smoke that was rising from some burning coconut shells.

Olifat didn't become mean when he got older; he was *born* nasty. He had to travel through the three lower levels of heaven to reach his father and managed to cause total havoc on the way. On the first three levels, children were having fun playing with the friendly and harmless fish they kept as pets, but Olifat soon put an end to that by making their scorpion fish sprout spikes, their gentle sharks grow razor-sharp teeth, and their stingrays develop painfully poisonous stingers.

When Olifat finally reached the fourth level, he saw a group of workers building a *färmal*, a house for the spirits of the dead. In these times, house builders in Micronesia had a special (and rather drastic) custom to ensure the new building's strength. As they were building it, they would kill someone and bury the body (or sometimes just the bloody head) in the bottom of one of the building's postholes before putting the posts in. Since the friends and family of the building's owner usually got more than a little upset when one of them was chosen to be sacrificed this way, people often killed and buried any strangers who were unlucky enough to be passing by at that particular time.

This custom was also followed in the sky world, and when the workers saw the strange boy wandering around, they figured he'd be the perfect victim for their posthole. Olifat may have been mean, but he certainly wasn't dumb. The men threw him down into the posthole, but seconds before they rammed the heavy post down into the hole to kill him, he quickly dug out a hollow cave off to one side and pressed himself into it. Confident that the boy was dead, the workers went off to finish their building.

Olifat, in the meantime, talked some termites into helping him tunnel through the post and up through the building's rafters. Suddenly the workers heard weird laughter and when they looked up they were astounded to see the boy they were sure they had murdered, perched in the rafters above them. Then, just in time or they would have killed him for sure, Olifat's father, Lugeiläng, showed up and ordered him to come down.

That was just the first of many times in which people would try to kill the trickster Olifat, and it was usually because he was such an infuriating and aggravating fellow. He was able to get away with so much mischief partly because he could transform himself into everything from insects and animals to coconut leaves and piles of dung. In one very strange story, he turned himself into a mosquito so he could be swallowed by his brother's wife in her drinking water. Nine months later he traumatized the whole family by being born as her son.

People blamed Olifat for everything from spoiling their food to stealing their wives, and most of the time they were right in their suspicions. His most vicious prank, however, was the murder of his own brother. It turned out that his father, the sky god Lugeiläng, had kept it secret from Olifat that he had a son by his first wife before he left heaven to marry Olifat's mother on earth. When Olifat discovered this brother everyone had kept hidden from him, he vowed revenge. This other son lived on the third level of heaven, but Olifat learned that each night after the boy came home from fishing, he proudly brought his catch up to show his father. Olifat crept up on him one night, chopped off his head, and then left it at his father's doorstep in place of his brother's usual nightly offering of fish.

Lugeiläng, of course, was outraged. He immediately restored his son's head to his body and breathed life back into him, but when he yelled at Olifat for his heinous act, Olifat just looked surprised and said how could he have killed someone who didn't exist?

Lugeiläng promptly kicked Olifat out of the sky world and that was the beginning of a long war that Olifat waged single-handed upon the heavens. To make his father and the other gods angry, he stole the secrets of fire and other immortal knowledge from them and brought them down to earth to give to humans. Finally, in an effort to make peace, Lugeiläng allowed Olifat to make his home in the god's sky palace. Olifat accepted, but still only spent half his time there. The other half he spent on earth tormenting (but also helping) humans.

The Tricksters of Oceania

Some areas of Oceania have creation myths, others assume the universe was always just there. Some cultures in Melanesia trace their ancestors back to spiritually powerful animals such as the crocodile or snake, while some Polynesian myths tell stories of heroic ancestors who made fantastic voyages to faraway places like the Sun, the Moon, and the Underworld. But one aspect of mythology almost all the islands of Oceania have in common is the concept of the trickster hero.

In Polynesia, it's the famous trickster hero Maui who battled the gods on behalf of mankind. In Melanesia, which is made up of an incredible number of small, isolated mountain communities, many of the stories are the same, but the names of trickster heroes vary from village to village. Here you can find the humorous adventures of Qat, Takaro, and To Kabinaba. In Micronesia, a constellation of tiny islands north of Melanesia, most of the stories have to do with worshipping divine ancestors, which included fish gods and the spider trickster hero Nareau. Other popular trickster heroes in Melanesia are Motitik and Olofat.

Throughout Oceania, trickster legends were handed down from generation to generation orally, by way of highly respected poets and storytellers. Australia's Aborigines passed on their hero myths orally too, but they also used rock, sand, cave, and bark paintings to illustrate their Dreamtime stories.

The vivid Aboriginal Dreamtime stories of the Giant Rainbow Serpent were often painted on walls of caves such as this one on Wessel Isle off the coast of Australia.

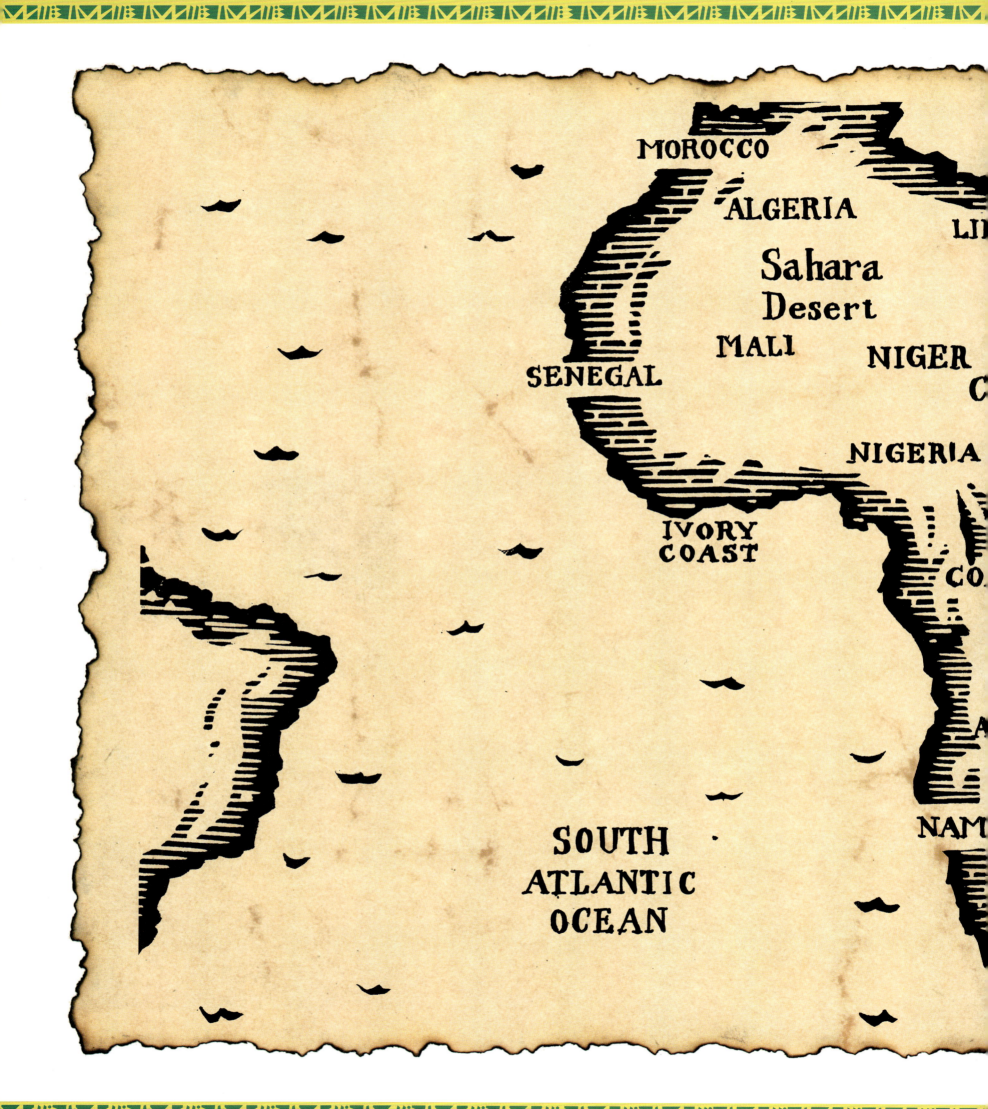

Chapter 7

Heroes of African Mythology

In African cultures, the rich oral tradition of storytelling has been passed down from generation to generation for thousands of years. The stories have taken many forms, from creation myths, hero legends, and adventure tales to proverbs, animal fables, songs, poems, and even riddles. And there are thousands and thousands of them. Not only do these stories still thrive in African cultures today, they have been transplanted to many other nations as well, especially those in the Western Hemisphere. Many of the folktales of black America and the Caribbean (such as Brer Rabbit and Uncle Remus) are rooted in this rich and vivid African heritage.

Anansi the Spider
A Tale of a West African Trickster Hero

Long ago the first spider, Anansi, traveled throughout the world on his web strings—although he sometimes looked and acted more like a wise old man than a spider. In that long-ago time, things were dull because there were no stories on earth for people to tell. The sky god, Onyame, kept all the stories for himself, locked away in a wooden box high in the sky. Anansi yearned to be the owner of all these stories so that he could know why and how all things existed. So did many others. Many people had offered to buy the stories from the sky god, but the price had proved too high for even the richest families.

Nevertheless, Anansi was determined to have them. When the sky god saw the thin, old spider, Anansi, climbing up his web to ask for the stories, he laughed at him. "What makes you think that you, of all creatures, can pay the price I'm asking?" he said.

"Well, tell me the price and we'll see," said Anansi.

Onyame said the only way he'd part with the stories was if someone brought him the three most fearsome creatures: Mmoboro, the nasty, swarming hornets; Onini, the python that swallowed men whole; and Osebo, the leopard who had teeth like spears. Anansi replied, "No problem. I will bring them."

Bowing, the spider quietly turned and crept back down his web through the clouds. First he devised a plan to capture Mmoboro, the nasty hornets. He filled a large, hollowed-out gourd with water, and then went walking through the bush until he saw the swarm of hornets hanging in a tree. He sprinkled some of the water out all over their nest. Then he poured the rest all over himself and covered his head with a large leaf. Still dripping, he called out to the hornets, "The rain has come, you foolish hornets, why don't you do as I do and protect yourself from the storm?" "Where will we go?" they asked. "Just fly inside this dry hollow gourd," he advised them.

The hornets thought it was a good idea and flew into the gourd. Anansi quickly plugged the hole, spun a thick web over the opening, and then took it to Onyame.

The sky god accepted the hornets Anansi brought him but said, "You have two more to go." Next Anansi set about to capture the

Leopards were popular characters in the animal fables of the Nigerian Obas.

120 Heroes of African Mythology

One of the most famous trickster figures in African mythology is the West African character known as Eshu to the Yoruba and as Elegba or Legba in Benin. A homeless, wandering spirit, he is said to be responsible for all quarrels between human beings and between humans and gods.

Heroes of African Mythology **121**

West Africans often attributed the invention of agriculture to a divine animal figure like the primordial antelope represented by this Malinke mask.

python that swallowed men whole. First, he cut off a long branch from a palm tree and gathered some strong vines. Then, as he walked to the swampy stream carrying these things, he began arguing out loud with himself, "This branch *is* longer than he is!—you lie, it is not!—no, it's true, this branch is longer!—no way, he's longer, *much* longer!"

The python, who couldn't help overhearing, asked "What are you muttering, Anansi?"

"My wife and I have been arguing," he replied. "She says that you are longer than this palm branch and I say that you are not."

Onini, the python, said, "Well there's an easy way to find out. Come over here and lay that branch down next to me and we will see if your wife is a liar or not."

So Anansi put the palm branch next to the python's body and watched as the large snake stretched himself out alongside it. Then quick as a flash, Anansi wrapped the vines around and around the python until he had the snake tied firmly to the branch. Anansi spun a web around the bound-up snake and dragged him back through the clouds to the sky kingdom. On seeing the gigantic snake, Onyame merely said, "There is still one thing more to go."

So Anansi came back to earth to find the next creature, Osebo the leopard, who had teeth like spears. After following the tracks of the leopard to see where he hunted, Anansi dug a very deep pit, which he disguised with branches. When he returned the next morning, he found Osebo the leopard pacing nervously on the bottom of the pit. Anansi told the leopard that if he crawled up the side as far as he could, he'd give him a hand and help him out, but as soon as Osebo got within reach, Anansi hit him over the head and pushed him back into the pit. Anansi quickly spun a tight web around the unconscious leopard and then carried his final trophy back to the sky god.

This time Onyame was impressed. He called together all of his nobles and told them how Anansi the Spider had done what no one else had been able to do. Then he announced in a loud voice that rang through the sky, "For now and forever, all my stories belong to you, Anansi. I give them to you with all my blessings, and from now on they will be called "spider stories."

Heroes of Animal Fables

Animal fables have always been one of the most popular forms of African storytelling. While some of these are just silly stories to entertain young children, most have a purpose. Animals are often portrayed with human weaknesses (like envy, gluttony, or greed) and the fables offer their listeners a moral, such as "Be very careful what you wish for—because you just might get it!" In many fables, an animal hero like the Hare or the Tortoise may be smaller and weaker than his elephant, rhinoceros, and crocodile neighbors, but with patience and cunning, he can often outwit them. They become appealing characters the listener can identify with, because no one likes to be pushed around or taken advantage of.

There is a Yoruba story, for example, in which both the Elephant and the Hippopotamus are angry with the Hare, unfairly claiming that he stole their food. The Hare calms the Elephant down by handing him one end of a rope and promising him that all he has to do is pull and he'll find a great treasure chest on the other end of the rope. Then the Hare walks through the woods to the river, hands the other end of the rope to the Hippopotamus, and tells him the same thing. The two huge animals pull and strain against each other for hours, each thinking they'll be pulling in a treasure, while the delighted Hare hops between them egging them on. Eventually the two animals get tired and the thirsty Elephant lumbers down to the river for a drink. When he compares notes with the panting Hippopotamus, they angrily realize they've been had, but by this time the laughing Hare has long since run off to safety.

Animal fables are also often used to explain natural phenomenon. There's a story told in

The animal pranksters found in so many African cultures like Hare, Mantis, and Anansi the Spider are heroes because they outwit more powerful animals such as elephants and hyenas and trick them into helping humans.

Heroes of African Mythology 123

Sierre Leone about how the leopard got its spots. It tells how Leopard and his wife were very friendly and often visited their neighbor, Fire. They begged Fire to visit them in return, but Fire never came. Finally, Fire agreed that if they created a road of dry leaves right up to the door of their house, he would come. They did, and sure enough, Fire soon came to visit them. But when Leopard and his wife opened the door, the wind whipped Fire's fingers of flame toward them. They managed to escape just before their house burned down, but as you can see, to this day their bodies are still marked with black spots where the fingers of Fire touched them.

Thousands of other fables explain things like why bats hang upside down and only fly at night, why snakes shed their skin, why rams paw the ground, why frogs swell up and croak, why spiders got to be bald, and why crocodiles don't die underwater.

One of the most popular animal heroes is Anansi the Spider, a trickster character in the folklore of many African cultures. He sometimes has names like Mr. Spider or Kwaku (Uncle) or Gizo (as the Hausa call him), but he's still the same rascally hero of hundreds of stories and fables. Although Anansi the Spider can be wise and sympathetic, more often he's characterized as a greedy, gluttonous, and cunning prankster. Either way, he is endlessly preoccupied with outwitting everybody and everything around him. Often the stories are about his frequent encounters with Onyame, the supreme sky god, and are told to explain the beginnings of certain natural phenomena (how the moon came into being, for example) or how certain customs and traditions got started (how men came to use hoes or why humans were given tongues). Many of the stories are morality fables in which Anansi's antics and weaknesses only get him into trouble.

This warrior has put his knife to good use. In African mythology, a divine blacksmith often plays a crucial role by stealing fire from the gods and teaching humans how to fashion tools and weapons.

Ogbe Baba Akinyelure, Warrior of Ibode
A Yoruba Myth from Nigeria

There was a time when war raged throughout the land and people knew the names of many great warrior heroes. But no man was more famous than Ogbe, a warrior who lived in the town of Ibode in the west. In those times, people believed that a warrior should never drink palm wine when his country was at war because it made his arms heavy, slowed his spear, and clouded his judgment. Ogbe, however, believed that he was so strong and skilled a warrior that it was fine for him to drink. It was even fine for him to ride into battle with the warmth of palm wine inside him. Because he was such a great hero, no one dared to say out loud that he shouldn't.

Ogbe had many wives and children in Ibode, but he loved his son Akinyelure the best, perhaps because Akinyelure's mother was Ogbe's most beloved wife. He loved his son so much that after the boy was born he changed his own name to Ogbe Baba Akinyelure (Ogbe, Father of Akinyelure).

One day the town held a great festival in honor of one of Ogbe's victories. The drumming, dancing, and singing went on all day and far into the night, and Ogbe drank many cups of wine. Very early the next morning a messenger came to the town and woke everyone with the news that an enemy force was rapidly approaching. As Ogbe and the town's other warriors took up their weapons and prepared for battle, young Akinyelure announced that this time he too would go along to fight the enemy. His father looked at him and decided that maybe he really was old enough to fight. Ogbe handed his son a spear and battle-ax and told him that they would proudly fight side by side. Without letting Akinyelure's mother know her son was going along, Ogbe and the other warriors went out to meet the enemy.

The battle was great and glorious. Hour after hour Ogbe and Akinyelure fought side by side until finally the enemy began to tire. When one of the warriors cried out that the enemy was fleeing into the bush, Ogbe, delighted, turned to look. It was only then that he noticed that Akinyelure was no longer at his side. He searched frantically across the fields until he found the body of his dead son, then dropped to the ground beside him in grief and despair.

The other warriors tried to convince Ogbe to return with them to Ibode, but he refused. How could he go back and face the dear wife whose son he had allowed to die? He said he would stay where he was because there was now nowhere else for him to go. As Ogbe said those words, he took root where he stood and turned into an iroko tree. But the great hero was never forgotten by the townspeople. Every year they came out to the field and laid sacrifices at the foot of the iroko tree in his memory.

Akokoaa and the Monster Sasabonsam
A Sefwi Tale from Ghana

A weary hunter was about to head home after wandering all day without firing so much as a single shot when he saw an antelope. He shot and killed it and was about to tie up the carcass with some vines when he heard a voice behind him. "Hunter," it said, "cut off the animal's legs."

When the hunter turned around he was horrified to see a gigantic, thin man with hair that reached down to his knees and teeth like red-hot spears. The monster's eyes were huge balls of fire that flashed when he again ordered the terrified hunter to cut off the animal's legs. After the hunter did what he was told, the monster Sasabonsam picked up the rest of the carcass and swallowed it whole, leaving only the legs for the hunter to take home.

The same thing happened the next day, the day after that, and the day after that. The hunter never told his pregnant wife what was happening, however, and she started to get a little angry and suspicious about her husband only coming home from his hunts with legs. She wanted to know what was happening to the rest of the meat. So she devised a plan to spy on him. She pounded a tiny hole in his powder box, and

Yoruba artists from Northern Yorubaland in Nigeria carved wooden figures and often decorated shrines representing female fertility myths.

Heroes of African Mythology 125

then filled it with ashes, and when he set out the next morning for his usual hunting grounds, all she had to do was follow the trail of ashes he left behind.

She was hiding behind a tree, watching, when her husband shot and killed a small black duiker antelope. She jumped about a foot when she heard the ghastly voice tell her husband to cut off the animal's legs. But this time Sasabonsam was not pointing at the animal the hunter had just killed but to the tree she was hiding behind. The hunter thought for a moment that a stray bullet must have killed a second animal—until he looked behind the tree and saw his wife, who had fainted from shock.

Smoke poured out of Sasabonsam's mouth as he again demanded the hunter cut off her legs. When the hunter didn't move, he angrily picked her up himself and was about to swallow her whole when her belly opened and her baby jumped out. The child's name was Akokoaa Kwasi Gyinamoa and he grew so fast that in a flash he was a smoke-breathing monster as big as Sasabonsam himself. Howling, the two began to fight over the woman's body. In their terrible fight, they uprooted trees and scattered all the wildlife in the forest. Finally, in a moment when Sasabonsam was trying to catch his breath, the child-giant grabbed the monster's magic hammer from his belt and hit Sasabonsam on the head three times.

Fatally wounded, Sasabonsam fell full-length on the ground and immediately turned into a great river. As for Akokoaa, he shrank back down to infant size, crawled back into his mother's womb, and patiently waited there to be born.

A Dogon village in Mali.

The Legend of Samba Gana
A Fulbe Tale from the Upper Niger Valley

There once was a very beautiful and wise princess named Annallja Tu Bari. Many knights came to seek her hand in marriage but soon left when they heard what she demanded of them. Her father had owned all the farming villages in the area until the day a warrior from a neighboring village challenged him to a duel for possession of the town. Annallja Tu Bari's father lost both his life and the town in that duel. Annallja Tu Bari wanted revenge.

In her anger and grief, Annallja demanded that any suitor who wanted a chance to marry her had to not only win back the town her father had lost, but conquer eighty other towns and villages in the surrounding area as well. Since that meant, in effect, mounting an all-out war, no one particularly cared to take her up on her offer. Years passed and Annallja remained unmarried

126 Heroes of African Mythology

This man is wearing the traditional dress of Niger. The cultures of the Upper Niger Valley, including the Yoruba, Bambara, and Dogon, developed some of the richest cosmologies of the world, with creation myths rivaling those of India and Mesoamerica in grandeur and subtlety.

Africa is home to an enormous diversity of cultures, and its peoples speak more than 1,000 different languages. Many, especially those along the Upper Niger River, have tenaciously preserved their myths and legends.

but grew more beautiful—and more melancholy—with every passing year. Her sadness affected everyone around her, and soon no one in her kingdom ever laughed.

In Faraka, a land far away, there lived a prince called Gana who had a strong and courageous son named Samba Gana. It was the custom in this land that when a son came of age, he would take his bards and servants and set out to find (and fight for) his own land. Samba Gana set out on his journey with great joy and laughter. Each town he came to, he challenged the prince who owned it and then fought with him until the prince conceded defeat. But Samba Gana always gave back what he had won. He not only let each vanquished prince live, he also let him keep his town. Samba Gana just laughed and went on his way.

One day when he was camped along the Niger River, one of his bards sang him a song about a sad and lovely princess named Annallja Tu Bari who would only marry the man who could conquer eighty towns and make her laugh. Samba Gana immediately sprang to his feet and demanded that they set off at once to find her. When they did, he saw that she was indeed incredibly beautiful—and incredibly sad. After getting a list of the towns she wanted conquered, Samba Gana instructed his bards to spend every day that he was gone singing to her about the land of Faraka and its noble heroes. They even sang to her about the great and terrible serpent of the Issa Beer that made the river rise and flood the land so that one year the people had too much rice and the next they went hungry.

As Annallja Tu Bari was learning everything there was to know about Faraka, one by one Samba Gana conquered all eighty of the towns on her list. Soon she ruled over all the princes and the knights in the land and when Samba Gana returned, she agreed to be his wife. But he said, "Why don't you laugh? I will not marry you until you laugh." She explained that, before she could not laugh because of her grief and anger; now she could not laugh because people in his Kingdom were hungry. She said the way she could ever laugh again was if he conquered the serpent of Issa Beer that caused so many people to suffer.

So Samba Gana set out to conquer the terrible serpent. When he finally found him on the Upper Niger, the fight was long and difficult. They fought for eight long years, and as they struggled the waters of the Niger churned and overflowed its banks. Mountains collapsed, and the earth opened up in yawning chasms. It took Samba Gana eight hundred broken lances and eighty swords, but he finally did conquer the serpent. But Annallja Tu Bari still wasn't satisfied. She sent word that Samba Gana was to bring her the subdued serpent so she could have it as her slave. Only then, she said, would she laugh.

This time Annallja Tu Bari had gone too far. When Samba Gana heard her final demand, he said she asked too much. He took his sword and stabbed the serpent in the heart, killing it. Samba Gana laughed one last time and then plunged the same bloody sword into his own breast.

Horrified when she heard the news of his death, Annallja summoned all her knights and rode with them night and day until they reached Samba Gana's bloody body on the banks of the river Niger. She ordered her people to build him the highest, most magnificent tomb that was ever built for any hero, a tomb so huge that it took thousands of workers eight years to build. When it was finally finished, Annallja Tu Bari climbed to the very top. As she stood on top, she commanded her knights and princes to spread all over the world and become heroes as great as her Samba Gana had been. Then she actually laughed—just once—and died. Her people

Twins play an important part in the creation myths of many African cultures including the Yoruba, Dogon, and Bambara of the Upper Niger Valley.

buried her beside Samba Gana in his burial chamber.

Heroes of African Mythology **129**

Aiwel Longar and the Spear Masters
A Dinka Legend from the Upper Nile

In a time long ago, lions held great dances and often invited people to attend. One night a young man was in the middle of a rather wild dance when a lion decided that he liked the man's bracelet. The lion demanded that the man give it to him and, when he refused, the lion bit the man's thumb off and he quickly bled to death. The young man left behind an infant daughter but no son, which saddened his grieving young widow even more. When a river spirit found her weeping on the riverbank, he told her she would have a son if she rolled up her skirts and waded in the river.

What the river spirit had promised soon came true, and the woman named her new son Aiwel. The baby was born with a full set of teeth, a sure sign of spiritual power, and it was soon obvious he had other powers as well. One day his mother left Aiwel asleep on the floor in the care of his sister. When she returned home, the large gourd in which she kept his milk was empty. She punished her daughter for drinking it, but in fact it was the infant Aiwel who drank it, not the girl. When the same thing happened three days in a row, the mother became suspicious and only pretended to leave so she could spy on her son. When she caught him in the act, Aiwel warned her that if she told anyone about it she would die. But the woman just couldn't keep the secret and she soon died just as Aiwel had predicted.

After that, Aiwel left home and went to live with his father, the river spirit, where he stayed until he grew up. When he became a man the river spirit gave him a magnificent, multicolored ox named Longar, and from that day on Aiwel's name became Aiwel Longar. He built

As in other world cultures, African trickster heroes such as Hare and Anansi the Spider often taught humans the crucial skills they needed to farm and raise cattle. This illustration depicts a Dinka cattle farm.

himself a house in the village and made a good living tending the cattle that had belonged to his mother's first husband (the unfortunate man who had been bitten by the lion).

One year there was a terrible drought and people had a difficult time finding enough grass and water to feed their cattle. Many of their animals became thin and died, but not Aiwel's; his cattle were fat and strong. Angry and resentful, a few of the villagers decided to spy on Aiwel and find out how he was feeding and watering his herd. They followed him to where some tufts of scraggly, long-rooted grass were growing. The grass didn't look like much, but when Aiwel pulled clumps of it up by the roots, there was water underneath. When Aiwel saw them spying on him, he warned the villagers not to tell his secret to anyone else or they would die. Of course, as soon as they returned to their village the men told everyone else about their discovery, and, of course, by the next day they were dead.

Aiwel Longar then had a talk with the village elders and advised the remaining people of the town to leave their land and follow him. He pointed out that their cattle were sure to die anyway and if they came with him he would take them to a sacred land of endless pastures, plenty of water, and no death. But the elders didn't believe him, so Aiwel set out alone, crossing great mountains and rivers on his journey.

In the end, a few brave villagers were willing to make the journey after all. To these few, Aiwel taught prayers and gave special fishing and war spears. He showed them the spiritual path. It was these trusted few, it is said, who became the first "spear masters," the elite clan of priests who, forever afterward, handed down their special powers and prayers to their children and to their children's children.

Kwasi Benefo's Journey to the Land of the Dead
An Ashanti Tale from Ghana

A long time ago there lived a young and prosperous Ashanti farmer named Kwasi Benefo who had flourishing fields and many cattle, but no wife to bear him children or care for his household. So Kwasi Benefo went looking for a wife. He soon fell in love with a village woman and they were married. They lived happily until one day his wife took ill and died. Grief-stricken, he dressed her in beads and a silk *amoise* (burial shroud) so she could be buried.

The Ashanti culture in the heart of Ghana's tropical rain forest has long been considered one of the best organized, most prosperous, and most influential cultures in Western Africa. It was traditionally the chief or odikro's *job to preserve traditional myths and customs.*

But Kwasi Benefo could not forget her. For a long time he missed her so much that his heart was no longer with the living. His brothers and friends implored him to go on with his life and find another woman to marry. At last, he did. They married and they too lived happy, contented lives until she became ill during her first pregnancy and died. He dressed his second wife in beads and a silk amoise and buried her.

Kwasi Benefo no longer wanted to live. For a long time, he would not even go out of his house. It took a long time for friends and family to convince him he should try to get over his grieving and go on with his life. The family of his second wife were so saddened by his suffering that they offered him their only other daughter as a wife in consolation. After a while, Kwasi Benefo let himself be persuaded and he and the young woman were married. Soon he came to love his new wife as much as he had loved the first two. He returned to tending his fields and cattle and they lived contented, prosperous lives. When he and his third wife announced the birth of a baby boy a year later, the village celebrated with much dancing and singing. Life was good.

But one day when he was working out in his fields, people from the village came to him with terrible news. His wife had gone down to the river to fetch water, they said, and on the way back, as she stopped to rest, a tree suddenly fell over and killed her. Numb with grief, Kwasi Benefo dressed his wife in her burial garments. After the funeral, he abandoned his farm and went off to live a meager, miserable life in the bush, barely staying alive on roots and seeds. Years passed and he had been alone so long he nearly forgot his name. But little by little his grief subsided and the desire for life came back to him once again. He cleared some new fields and began to farm again. After a while he was again a prosperous farmer and began to yearn for a wife and children.

Kwasi Benefo married a fourth time. It was not long before this wife, too, took ill and died. Now he was beyond despair. That night he as he lay sleepless, the thought came to him that he should go to Asamado, the Land of the Dead, so he could be with the four young women he had loved. So he went to Nsamandow, the cemetery where his dead wives were buried, and from there groped his way through a pitch black, silent forest until he came to a dimly lit spot on

The akuaba, or wooden doll, on the left was carved in the image of the Ashanti moon goddess Nyame, a symbol of revered womanhood and the fullness of life. The Yoruba ibeji figurines on the right represent twins, a favorite mythological theme of many African cultures.

132 Heroes of African Mythology

a riverbank. On the far bank opposite him sat an old woman washing women's beads and burial amoises in a large brass pan. Kwasi knew at once she was Amokye, the welcomer of the souls of dead women to Asamado. The dead gave her their beads and burial shrouds when crossing the river.

Amokye told him to go away, that he was a living soul and therefore not allowed to pass to the other side. But when he told her the sad story about the deaths of his four beloved wives, she took pity on him and allowed him to cross just long enough to speak to their spirits. Kwasi Benefo crossed the river and walked until he came to a house where he heard his wives singing him a song of welcome. Since they were invisible, he could not see them, but as they prepared him dinner and laid it on the table before him, they soothed him with their gentle and loving voices. They sang to him of how much they loved him and what a good and kind husband he had been to each of them. Then they told him that one day, after he died, they would all be together in this spirit world, but that now he had to return to the world and go on living. They advised him to get married yet one more time, promising that this time his wife would not die. Hearing those sweet words from the women he loved, Kwasi Benefo lay down and fell into a deep sleep.

When he awoke he was no longer in the land of Asamado but in the forest. He made his way back to the village and began to rebuild his house and fields. Not long after that he met a young woman from a neighboring village and asked her to marry him. Kwasi Benefo and his new wife had many children and lived a long and happy life.

The Dogon artists of Mali, in western Africa, have long been famous for their carved wooden sculptures of mythological female figures known as tellem.

Heroes of African Mythology 133

Chapter 8

Heroes of Central and South American Mythology

It's believed that the peoples who settled the Americas are the descendants of groups who migrated across the Bering Strait more than 30,000 years ago. They spread south and east across the North American continent, eventually pushing their way down through Mexico and Central and South America until they reached Tierra del Fuego.

Many of the groups remained small communities of hunters, fishermen and food gatherers. Their relatively simple cultures developed mythologies with local, mostly human characters. The stories often concerned themselves with rites of passage such as birth, reaching puberty, marriage, and death. But a few of the groups, like the Aztecs, Mayans, Toltecs, Olmecs, and Incas, developed highly organized cultures with complex mythologies.

Whether simple or complex, almost all the cultures had some mythological themes in common. For example, most worshipped the sun, most had myths that told of a great and devastating flood, and many revered the jaguar as a powerful mythological figure.

The Flight of Quetzalcoatl
An Aztec Legend from Mexico

Quetzalcoatl, the "feathered serpent," was both a god and a hero to people in parts of Mexico and Central America for many centuries. Legend has it that he was the one who taught people the fine arts of smelting silver and setting precious stones, sculpting statues, and writing in books with hieroglyphics. He taught them how to keep accurate clocks and calendars by studying the sun and the planets and how to build magnificent temples. He was also the one who taught people about *maize* (corn).

The story goes that when Quetzalcoatl first arrived, the people were half starved because they only had roots to eat. Quetzalcoatl turned himself into a black ant to burrow into the mountainside where maize was hidden and then laboriously dragged the kernels back to the villagers so they would have crops to grow and food to eat.

But of all the arts he taught his people, one in particular was lacking. He refused to teach them the art of war. While other peoples in Mexico and Central America were making bloody sacrifices to the gods by tearing out the hearts of living men and women, Quetzalcoatl wanted only offerings of bread, flowers, perfumes, and butterflies. There are stories that tell how demons tried repeatedly to trick him, even getting him drunk, so that he would declare war on neighboring civilizations and order human sacrifices. But he never yielded or consented because he loved his people too much to put them in jeopardy.

Quetzalcoatl dressed in the magnificent plumage of colorful bird feathers and lived in a huge silver and gold house set with precious stones as bright and colorful as himself. He kept flocks of beautiful birds around his house that

The Aztec hero Quetzalcoatl was depicted not only as the feathered or plumed serpent god shown in this codex, but as the wind god Ehecatl, the benevolent god of learning and crafts, and the god of twins.

Here Quetzalcoatl personified as an eagle joins the figure of Quetzalcoatl as a feathered snake to depict the rising morning star, the planet Venus.

filled the air for miles around with their sweet songs. Quetzalcoatl's house stood on the outskirts of Tollan, overlooking maize fields where the stalks grew so big that a man could only carry one cob at a time. And there were astonishing cotton fields where the cotton grew thick and fluffy and was already colored in vibrant shades of red, yellow, blue, and black, so that no one had to dye the cotton before making it into cloth. Inside the house were many fiercely loyal dwarves who attended Quetzalcoatl.

Because of Quetzalcoatl, the people were prosperous and happy. Life was good for a long time—that is, until the day that Tezcatlipoca showed up. Tezcatlipoca was an evil sorcerer who wandered all over the earth stirring up strife and war among men, getting them to kill each other and destroy the countryside. Now he was after the peace-loving god-king Quetzalcoatl.

Tezcatlipoca was crafty and his ways were often subtle. First he frightened everyone in the city by causing thick spiderwebs to descend upon it. Then he rode down from the mountain on a blast of wind so cold that all the bright flowers shriveled up and died. When Quetzalcoatl felt the coldness, he knew it meant that Tezcatlipoca was out to get him; he told his servants that it would be better if he left before all of Tollan was destroyed. After all, it wasn't the people of Tollan that Tezcatlipoca was really after.

His servants watched in despair as Quetzalcoatl burned down his silver and gold house with all the precious stones. Suddenly, Tezcatlipoca appeared beside him and challenged Quetzalcoatl to a ball game. All the people of Tollan came to the stadium to watch the game, the object of which was to score points by successfully throwing a large ball through a ring mounted high on one wall of the court.

No one really expected Tezcatlipoca to play fair. As Quetzalcoatl caught the ball and turned to shoot it up at the ring, Tezcatlipoca transformed himself into a vicious jaguar and sprang at him. Quetzalcoatl fled the stadium, running as fast as he could with Tezcatlipoca hot on his heels. The jaguar chased him through the streets of the city and out into the countryside before he lost him in the maize fields. But Quetzalcoatl knew he had to keep running if he wanted to stay alive.

Quetzalcoatl's loyal dwarves knew their master was no longer a young man and that the running would soon exhaust him. They knew where he would be hiding and ran to join him. The dwarves guarded Quetzalcoatl as he rested, and when he went on, they played music on their flutes to give him heart. Even so, whenever he looked back at Tollan in the valley below, he wept with grief.

There were two mountains Quetzalcoatl had to cross if he hoped to escape: the Fire Mountain and the Mountain of Snow. He and his followers managed to make it across the Fire Mountain, but the Mountain of Snow was so bitterly cold that all of his dwarves died. Brokenhearted, Quetzalcoatl stood on the mountaintop for hours wailing a sad song of bereavement for his noble friends.

He descended the other side of the Mountain of Snow alone and made his way, finally, to the seashore. One version of the legend says that here he made a raft of snakes and sailed out to sea until he came to the Land of Tlappallan in the Country of the Sun, where he found the Water of Immortality. The legend prophesied that he would return someday as a magnificent young warrior.

Another version tells how some of the dwarves survived the Mountain of Snow after all and reached the seashore with him. There Quetzalcoatl dressed himself in his best robes and feathers and asked his loyal servants to build him a funeral pyre, upon which he threw himself and was consumed in flames. They say that a flock of birds flew into the fire and rescued Quetzalcoatl's heart. They took it high up into the heavens where he was reborn as the planet Venus. If you look hard into the night sky, you can see still see him sitting upon his throne.

right
The legends of Quetzalcoatl are carved into the great stone temple at Tenochtitlán.

opposite
Because people depended on the cultivation of maize (corn) for food, almost every Mexican culture had maize fertility deities such as the Mayan god Ah Mun and the Aztec gods Chicomecoatl and Centeotl.

Anthropologists continue to search for the origins of the Quetzalcoatl myth—are the myths based on the story of a real man?

Quetzalcoatl, from the city of Tula in the twelfth century. As for the mystical prophecy that Quetzalcoatl would someday return, the belief was so strong that when the first Spaniard, Hernán Cortés, landed in 1519, the Aztecs believed that he was their returning hero and therefore did not defend themselves against the Spanish onslaught until it was too late. It's hard to blame them. The conquistador Cortés not only fit the description of their light-skinned, resplendent god-king, he arrived on the exact calendar day of Quetzalcoatl's birth, the date of the prophesied return.

The Twins of Popol Vuh
A Mayan Tale from Mexico

God or Human?

The god-king Quetzalcoatl was worshiped in Mexico as early as A.D. 300 and over the centuries was adopted by both the Aztec and the Mayan cultures. But historians have had a hard time separating myth from fact. The Quetzalcoatl legends are often confusing because the name Quetzalcoatl was adopted over the centuries by several actual human rulers and many of their heroic exploits are interwoven into the god myths. For example, historians believe that the myth of Quetzalcoatl's flight and disappearance from Mexico probably refers to a real event, the driving out of a priest-king who was actually named Topiltzin, but who called himself

According to the ancient *Popol Vuh* or "council book" (which was first transcribed from hieroglyphics into Spanish in the sixteenth century by a Spanish friar) the gods made the earth with its land masses and bodies of water, then created plant life to cover it. At this point, there was still no sun; the only light came from the glow of the spirit powers within the water. The gods decided that they needed creatures on earth who would worship them, so they created mammals and birds. But instead of reciting prayers, all these animals did was hiss, bark, and cackle. So the gods decided to create humans.

The first time they used clay, but that was a disaster. Not only were these creatures soft and mindless, but they couldn't stand and they dissolved too easily in water. Next the gods tried wood. That was a little better because the men they formed could talk and multiply, but had neither souls nor minds. They immediately forgot all about their creators and started crawling around on all fours. These wooden men treated everything around them, including their dogs, so badly that the gods sent a great flood to destroy them. When that didn't work, they turned them into monkeys.

While the gods were figuring out what to try next, a dangerous and quite conceited impostor god appeared who claimed to be the sun, the light, and the moon all rolled into one. He was a giant with a gaudy, glittering face of silver and emeralds who called himself Gukup-Caquix. Sitting on his silver throne, he claimed to be so beautiful and so powerful that the whole earth actually lit up in his presence. (In reality he was an ugly and clumsy oaf.) It became obvious to the gods that before they could devote any more time to creating humans, they had to get rid of this intruder.

It was the twin-heroes Hunapú and Ixbalanqué who waged the war against Gukup-Caquix and finally defeated him. After spying on him for a while, the twins realized that the giant's weakness was food, especially the fruit of a certain tree. So they hid themselves in the forest and when the giant came for his daily meal, they shot him with arrows. Before he died, however, Gukup-Caquix managed to crawl home and tell his two sons, Zipacna and Caprakan, what had happened.

Zipacna and Caprakan demanded revenge for their father's death, and they turned out to be every bit as evil and intimidating as their father had been. Among their many heinous deeds was intoxicating four hundred young warriors and then crushing them to death—they did this just for the fun of it.

First the twins went after Zipacna. Just like his gluttonous father, Zipacna's weakness was food, and his special passion was hunting along the riverbanks for crabs; so the twins tied a long string to a fake crab and placed the crab at the entrance to a nearby cave. After luring Zipacna into the cave, they caved in the mountain and crushed him. The twins also used the food approach to kill Zipacna's brother, Caprakan. His weakness was succulent, golden-brown birds roasting on a spit. Unfortunately for him, he didn't realize until it was too late that

The Mayan sun god, Ahau Kin, was portrayed as both young and old. Between sunset and sunrise it was believed he journeyed through the underworld as the Jaguar God.

Heroes of Central and South American Mythology **141**

This Aztec mosaic mask represents the god Quetzalcoatl.

the twins had basted the birds with poison.

According to the *Popol Vuh*, the twins Hunapú and Ixbalanqué went on to have a number of heroic adventures in which they fought evil and avenged wrongs. By far the most famous and exciting of these exploits was their final victory—the day they defeated the gods of the underworld in a ball game.

Actually, it had all started many years before when the twin's father, Hun-Hunapú, had been lured to the underworld to play ball. The Xibalba, the lords of the underworld, had not only beaten him, they had cut off his head and hung it on a calabash tree as a warning to anyone else who might be brash enough to challenge them.

Hunapú and Ixbalanqué believed it was their duty to go down to the underworld and avenge their father's death; the best way to do that was to challenge the Xibalba to another ball game. The lords of the underworld accepted the challenge, but only on the condition that the twins first be subjected to a series of trials to prove their skill and courage.

They survived the first night in the pitch-black House of Gloom, mainly because they resisted the temptation to light the "cigars" they had been given. The next night they were shut up in the House of Knives, not only did they survive, they talked the knives and some friendly ants into cutting a bouquet of flowers which they gave to their captors the next morning. The next night, they lit fires to survive the House of Cold, and the night after that, fed magic bones to the hideous animals in the House of Jaguars to keep from being eaten alive. They even managed to live through their night in the House of Fire.

But they weren't quite so lucky when they reached the final trial, a night in the House of Bats. Here Hunapú was decapitated by one of the bats. Nevertheless, his twin Ixbalanqué managed to charm some of the other creatures living in the House of Bats, and convinced a turtle to climb up on his twin's shoulders and disguise himself as Hunapú's head so it would look as though he had never been decapitated. Then the brave brothers set off for the ball court to play the match as planned.

It was a very odd game. The twins pretended to play ball with the evil Xibalba as if nothing was wrong, even though the gods had suspended Hunapú's real head over the ball court with a rope. As the game got underway, one of the gods threw the ball at the head, but it bounced off into a corner where it startled a rabbit out of its hole. The gods were momentarily distracted by the rabbit and didn't notice how Ixbalanqué grabbed Hunapú's suspended head and swapped it with the turtle perched on Hunapú's shoulders.

The head reattached itself instantly and Hunapú was as good as new.

When the Xibalba realized what had happened they were dumbfounded at the power the twins had to repair themselves after they had been cut up. Obsessed with acquiring their secret ability, the gods asked the twins to perform on them too, so they could see how it was done. The twins gladly obliged them—except for one small detail. After they dismembered the Xibalba, they didn't bother to put them back together again.

In honor of their tremendous victory over the evil underworld, Hunapú and Ixbalanqué were reborn as the Sun and Moon and have bathed the new earthly world in light ever since.

Twins in Mythology

Humans were fascinated with twin births long before they developed religions. In the earliest cultures, the birth of twins was considered a very bad omen, and the faster the babies were killed, the better. A twin birth might foretell the coming of a famine (symbolic of too many mouths to feed and not enough food), for example, or be a sign from the gods that the parents had, perhaps unknowingly, violated strict tribal taboos and therefore should be punished.

But as cultures advanced, the custom of killing twins stopped and instead twins became much-revered symbols of fertility. Almost every culture in the world has at least one twin-heroes myth, including the Aztecs, Zunis, Ashantis, and Babylonians. The Greeks have Castor and Pollux as well as Helen and Clytemnestra; the Romans have Romulus and Remus. Early Egyptians and Ugandans believed the placenta was an incomplete twin that possessed a soul and was to be given a burial and treated with special respect. Some Native American cultures in the northwest United States have myths that tell how twins are actually salmon in human disguise.

In many cultures, the twins are both heroes, but in some, they are rivals. In some Iroquois legends, for example, one twin is a hero but the other is an evil trickster. Feuding twins who appear in the Bible include Jacob and Esau (twin sons of Isaac and Rebekah who even fought over who would be born first), and Jacob's fighting grandsons, Pharez and Zarah.

In Mexican and Central and South American cultures, doubleness in nature was often interpreted as a manifestation of the supernatural or as a divine intervention by the gods, which is why many of the Incan, Aztec, and Mayan gods (such as Quetzalcoatl) were twins or superhuman twins. They usually played the roles of warriors, builders, healers, or fertility symbols, and they were often the offspring of air, water, or thunder. Peruvian Indians once revered twin gods Apocatequil and Piquerao and believed they were responsible for thunder and lightning.

The Tauma Indians of Guyana have legends of twin heroes named Tuminikar and Duid. Tuminikar is the good and wise twin who does good deeds to help mankind, while his brother Duid is an idler who constantly plays tricks on him and tries to undo his good efforts.

In the Greater Antilles, the Taino Indians have an intriguing twin legend called the *Four Twins of One Birth* in which the four heroes have a number of cosmic adventures before settling down and creating mankind. The first man actually emerges from a neck tumor that one of the four twins develops after an old fisherman spits tobacco on him.

Another people whose legends attribute the creation of mankind to twin heroes are the Bakari Indians of Brazil. In addition to making the first men, the twins Keri and Kame also stole feather balls from a vulture and turned them into the sun and moon. They gave humans the gift of sleep by stealing a lizard's eyelids.

Another twin-heroes myth, this one from the Cariban cultures of the northern Venezuelan rain forests, is the *Cycle of the Twin Heroes*. Here the twin boys Shikiemona and Iureke steal fire from the Toad-Woman (by slitting her throat and letting it gush up from her belly where she kept it hidden) and then hide it in the wishu and kumnuatte trees for humans to find.

Even the Great Feathered Serpent Quetzalcoatl had a twin, the dog-headed god Xolotl. It is said that after the first humans had been wiped out in the four cosmic upheavals, the twin bothers descended to Mictlan (the underworld) to collect the human bones so they could resurrect them. But when they were fleeing from the Death Lord, they dropped the bones and they shattered. Picking up the pieces, Quetzalcoatl escaped and took them to the earth goddess Cihuacoatl (Snake Woman) who ground them into meal. Quetzalcoatl sprinkled his own blood on the meal and re-created the human race.

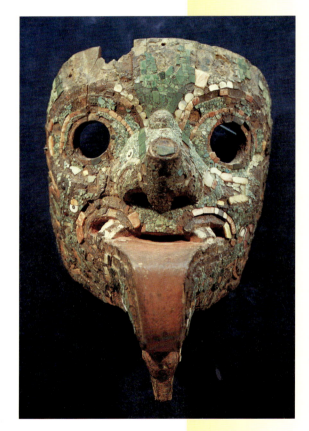

This Aztec mask represents Quetzalcoatl's evil twin named Xolotl, who tried to destroy the human race by collecting the bones of those who died from the underworld.

By the time of the Spanish conquest in 1532, the Inca emperor ruled a remarkably advanced empire that extended along the Andes and Pacific Coast from the northern border of present-day Ecuador in the north to central Chile in the south.

Heroes of Central and South American Mythology

El Dorado—The Kingdom of the Gilded Man
An Incan Legend from the Colombian Highlands

In parts of Mexico and Central and South America, people still whisper the legends of El Dorado, a mysterious country somewhere on the continent whose cities were paved with gold. The land was named El Dorado, or "gilded man," after its fabled priest-kings who were said to be covered from head to toe with gold dust. They and their country have eluded explorers for centuries.

Although later adopted by the Aztec, Mayan, and especially Incan cultures, the legend of El Dorado probably originated among the Chibcha Indians who inhabited the highlands around present-day Bogota, Colombia.

According to the story, El Dorado is such a wealthy country that not only are its streets paved with gold, but all the buildings in each of the cities are encrusted with emeralds and other precious stones. In spite of their wealth, however, the people of El Dorado are a spiritual people, and each new warrior who becomes the priest-king of El Dorado has to follow a strict traditional daily ritual.

It is said that the priest-kings of the fabled country of El Dorado were so wealthy they had their subjects smear them with resin and then gild them from head to toe in gold dust.

Every morning, the king's attendants anoint their ruler by smearing his body with resin and then blowing gold dust all over him through a tube. The king then goes about his daily business completely gilded with gold. In the evening, the king's attendants take him out on a fantastically decorated raft to the middle of sacred Lake Guatavita, where he dives into the water and washes off the gold as an offering to the gods. Meanwhile, all of the people lined up on shore throw their own offerings of gold and gems into the water.

The Spanish, who conquered the rich cities of the Incas and the Aztecs in the sixteenth century, became obsessed with the legend of El Dorado and went to great lengths to find the country and its gilded rulers. Many of the Spanish conquistadors, including Gonzalo Pizarro (brother of the man who conquered the Incas), spent years cutting through the pathless jungles and fevered swamps of the Amazon River valley in a vain search. Thousands of men died on these fruitless expeditions; hundreds of others contracted leprosy.

In 1569, a Spanish conquistador named Gonzalo Ximenes Quesada found what he believed to be the fabled Lake Guatavita in the mountain highlands of Colombia. He tortured several local Chibcha chieftains over a slow fire to find out where they were hiding their gilded priest-king—but with no success. Since then, countless explorers of every possible nationality have searched not only South America, but also Central America, Mexico, and even parts of the southwestern United States for the legendary land of El Dorado. In 1913, a British company even tried draining the lake Quesada in a fruitless effort to get at the riches they were convinced were at its bottom.

In Inca myths, a hero's journey often took him over the perilous and starkly beautiful Andes mountains.

The Strange Adventures of Alcavilu
A Tale Told by the Araucanian Indians of Chile

Alcavilu, the handsome son of a chieftain, was noble and wise even as a child. One day, when he was about sixteen, Alcavilu told his father that he longed to take a journey and find out what was beyond the great mountains that encircled their village. The chieftain was sad to see his son go, but gave him his blessing nevertheless. He also gave Alcavilu a fine horse with a silver saddle, a deerskin sack filled with food for his journey, and some magic leaves to ward off sickness and evil spirits.

With much excitement, Alcavilu waved goodbye to his father and set off alone on his journey. He rode through broad valleys and crossed bubbling streams until he came to a deep forest where he stopped to take his meal. Thinking he had to be the only person within hundreds of miles, Alcavilu was startled to hear the voice of an old man behind him, bidding him good day. The old man was dressed in such ragged garments that he shivered from the cold. Alcavilu quickly wrapped the old man in his blanket and offered him food.

After they had finished eating, the old man sat a long time without speaking, then told Alcavilu that he had looked into the boy's future and could foresee that he would have many strange adventures before returning home to his father—and that he would not return from his journey alone.

When the old man got up to leave, Alcavilu insisted that he take the horse with the silver saddle and a blanket because he obviously needed them more than Alcavilu would. In gratitude for his kindness, the old man gave Alcavilu a small, green magic leaf that gave the person who chewed it the power to understand the language of animals and birds. The boy thanked him and they went their separate ways.

Alcavilu set off on foot chewing the old man's magic leaf. He slept in the forest that night and, when he awoke, he saw a lion stretched out nearby. The lion spoke softly to

Heroes of Central and South American Mythology 147

him in a language the astonished Alcavilu could understand, saying that an old man had asked him to protect the boy as he journeyed through the forest. The lion then plucked a pure white hair from his chest and gave it to Alcavilu. He told him it was a magic hair, and that it would give Alcavilu the power to change himself into any bird or animal or to fly anywhere he wished in the world.

After he left the forest, Alcavilu held the pure white hair tightly in his fist, closed his eyes, and wished that he could go to some wondrous place he had never before visited. All of a sudden, he was standing on the rim of a great volcano. Loud roars and tremendous billows of smoke belched forth menacingly from the volcano's mouth. Alcavilu was amazed to see a cottage up there, and even more amazed to see a pale young girl standing in the doorway. "Run for your life!" she screamed. "If Cherufe, the god of the volcano, wakes up and finds you here, he will throw you into the crater!" When Alcavilu demanded to know why she didn't run away herself, she told him she was Cherufe's servant and had no choice but to stay. She pleaded with him to leave until he finally turned himself into a bird and flew away.

Alcavilu flew for many hours until he finally saw a small house in a meadow. He perched for a moment on a plant outside its door and was so tired that he fell fast asleep. The next thing he knew, a young girl had picked him up lovingly and put him in a cage in the kitchen to keep her company while her father and brothers worked out in the field. Every time she passed the cage, she whispered to her new pet, "I love you." The girl's name was Kallfury and she was so kind and so beautiful that Alcavilu immediately fell in love with her.

Later, when her father and brothers came in from the fields and sat down to dinner, Alcavilu could smell the delicious dinner that Kallfury had cooked and longed to join them at their table. That night he had an idea. First he turned himself into a tiny black ant to escape the

cage, then he turned himself back into a boy. He went to the cupboard and was just about to take a bite out of a piece of juicy leftover meat when the girl's father woke up and caught him. In seconds, the whole family was awake and demanding to know who he was and what he was doing there.

Alcavilu told them the whole story, and when he got to the part about the cabin at the mouth of the volcano, the father exclaimed that the girl he saw must be his long-lost other

above
Pipe and flute music and ceremonial dance still play an important part in the myth and ritual of Peruvian culture.

opposite
The Inca emperors built a vast system of roads to be used only by their powerful military force to control the empire. Warriors like the one in this painting were important members of the Inca culture.

daughter, Murtilla, who had been stolen by the volcano god months before and then hidden away where no one could find her. Alcavilu immediately volunteered to rescue her.

He changed himself back into a bird and flew off to the volcano, where he turned into a boy again just long enough to advise Murtilla of his plan. He told her that as soon as he turned himself into a lion, she was to climb on his back and hang onto his mane as hard as she could, no matter what happened. She obeyed him without a word. They could hear Cherufe snoring from inside the volcano as they fled.

When Alcavilu brought Murtilla back to her home, there was great rejoicing. The grateful father, however, was distraught because he was too poor to give Alcavilu the reward he so richly deserved. "There is only one gift I long to have," said Alcavilu, "and that is your daughter Kallfury's hand in marriage. I love her with all my heart!" Overjoyed, Kallfury rushed to her father's side and assured him that she had loved Alcavilu even when he was a bird.

Just then, they all heard a horse neighing in front of the cottage. It was the old man from the forest, returning Alcavilu's horse and blanket. In thanks, he had filled the saddlebags with gold and precious stones because he had known that Alcavilu would be needing a wedding present.

Alcavilu and Kallfury rode the horse back to his father's kingdom where the chieftain greeted them both with open arms. He gave them a magnificent wedding and many years later, when he died and Alcavilu took his place as ruler, he and Kallfury ruled the kingdom wisely and kindly for many long years.

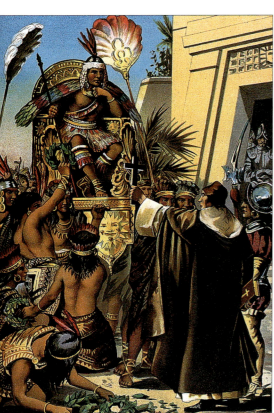

When the Spanish conquered the Incas in 1532, Catholic priests tried to suppress what they saw as native paganism. In most cases, the Incas either continued to practice their old beliefs or adopted a form of Catholicism that incorporated many of their old gods and spirits.

Using myths for political power

In large cultures such as the Inca and Aztec, rulers used mythology to reinforce their power over the people they conquered. Claiming to be gods themselves, or the descendants of gods, these rulers used often used existing myths and religious beliefs to justify the use of human sacrifice, which proved to be a very formidable and persuasive political tool.

Sometimes larger cultures like the Aztecs merged the beliefs of the people they conquered with their own, creating an even more complex mythology with hundreds of different gods. The most important and powerful of these gods had names like Tlaoc, Tezcatlipoca, Xipe Totec, Huitzilopochtli, and Quetzalcoatl.

In the isolated hunting and fishing communities of the Amazon basin in South America, it was often the shamans or medicine men who used myths for political power. People believed in a spirit world teeming with ogres, demons, and powerful spirits who could make both good and terrible things happen to people. They also believed it was only the shamans who had the special knowledge to communicate with those spirits—and thereby protect the people—through elaborate rituals.

Botoque Steals Fire from Jaguar's Wife
A Kayapo Tale from the Rain Forests of Brazil

In the beginning, because people did not possess fire, they had to eat their vegetables raw and warm their pieces of meat on rocks in the hot sun. One day a boy named Botoque and his older brother-in-law were out hunting for food when they spotted a macaw's nest high on a cliff. They quickly made a makeshift ladder out of some branches and vines and Botoque climbed up and reached the nest. In it he found two large eggs, which he carefully threw down to his brother-in-law; but on the way down, the eggs turned into stones and broke the young man's hands when he tried to catch them. Botoque's brother-in-law was so angry that he pushed away the ladder and left Botoque stranded on the cliff.

Botoque was up there many days before he finally saw a jaguar carrying a bow and arrow along with a pack full of game he had caught. The jaguar didn't see Botoque, but did see his shadow on the ground. Thinking it was some kind of animal, the jaguar pounced on the shadow before he realized his mistake. Feeling a little foolish and also taking pity on the stranded boy, the jaguar promised he wouldn't eat him and said he instead wanted to adopt him as a son. Botoque agreed, and the jaguar set the ladder back against the cliff so that the boy could climb back down.

The jaguar sincerely liked Botoque and gladly took him into his home, where the boy saw fire for the first time and ate the delicious meat that had been cooked over it. The jaguar's wife, however, was not so friendly. She hated Botoque, and whenever the jaguar was off hunting, she refused to give Botoque any of the meat she was roasting. One day she bared her claws so threateningly that Botoque fled and hid up in a nearby tree.

Although the jaguar scolded his wife and demanded that she treat Botoque better, she ignored his warnings and, as the days passed, became ever more hostile toward the boy. Finally, out of concern for the boy's life, the jaguar showed Botoque how to make a bow and arrow and how to use it to defend himself. The next time the jaguar's wife threatened the boy with her claws, he killed her. Then, horrified at what he had done, he grabbed the cooked meat, wrapped a burning ember from the fire in a deer pelt, and fled back to his own village.

Jaguar cults were popular throughout South America but especially in the Amazon basin. Shamans claimed they could magically transform themselves into these powerful predators to divine the future, bring death and destruction to their enemies, and protect villages from evil spirits.

When the men in the village saw the strange and wonderful things Botoque had brought back with him—the bow and arrows, the cooked meat, and the fire—they rushed out to the jaguar's house to steal some for themselves. Legend has it that the jaguar was so hurt and angry at the boy's ingratitude that he vowed to eat his food raw from then on, and to hunt only with his fangs and claws. To this day, if you look into a jaguar's mirror-like eyes, you can see the reflection of the fire he lost so very long ago.

Chapter 9

Heroes of Native North American Mythology

It's believed that the native peoples of North America migrated across the Bering Strait from Siberia more than 30,000 years ago. They spread south and eastward in small groups across the continent, with each group adapting to the particular area in which it settled. Some developed agricultural societies, some had cultures based on hunting or fishing. By the time the first Europeans arrived in the fifteenth century, there were more than five hundred unique cultures on the North American continent, each with its own language and mythological traditions.

Some basic themes were common to most or all of these many cultures. Almost all had myths that explained how the earth was created and where people came from. Animals who could change into human form whenever they chose often played an important part in these stories—trickster heroes who gave humans their laws and traditions or taught them skills such as weaving or planting corn.

Native Americans did not traditionally write down their myths, but passed them on by word of mouth. Certain members of the community were chosen as storytellers, often as much for their excellent memories as for their ability to tell good stories.

Coyote and the Giant
A Navajo Hero Legend

Coyote is one of the most loved and famous Native American cultural heroes and he can be found in the legends of Indian cultures throughout the Southwest, the West, and the Central Plains. In some, he is portrayed as a creator or a sorcerer, while in others he's a hero, a trickster, or even a lover. In the following Navajo myth, Coyote plays the trickster hero.

A very long time ago there were huge, evil giants who roamed the earth looking for little children to eat. One day, Coyote saw one of the giants skulking around the edge of a small village and decided he was going to teach him a lesson. Knowing how incredibly stupid these monsters were, Coyote convinced the giant that if he wanted a keen mind and the power to perform the magic that he himself had, he needed to take sweat baths. Coyote even offered to help build him his own sweat lodge.

After the lodge was built, Coyote and the giant heated large rocks and filled the interior with steam until it was hot enough for a good sweat bath. As he and the giant sat in the dark lodge, Coyote announced that he would demonstrate some of his magic. He would break his own leg, he said, and then instantly mend it again.

What they giant didn't know was that Coyote had hidden an unskinned deer leg in the back of the lodge when he wasn't looking. In the steamy darkness, Coyote took a rock and smashed the deer leg with a loud crack and then let the giant feel the skin and bone where it was broken. The giant was completely fooled—and very impressed.

right
According to the sacred teachings of the Navajo, or Diné, as they call themselves, when a person becomes ill, he or she is out of harmony with the universe. As part of the healing process, a Singer or medicine man may create a ceremonial sand painting near the patient using the sacred colors of white, yellow, black, blue, and red.

opposite
Because many Native American peoples in the Southwest depended on the cultivation of maize (corn) for food, hero myths were often about tricksters like Coyote who showed people how to raise and harvest it.

154 Heroes of Native North American Mythology

Heroes of Native North American Mythology 155

Then Coyote spat on the leg and cried out, "Leg, be whole again!" When the giant reached over and felt Coyote's real leg, he was astounded to find it whole and unbroken.

Coyote offered to repeat the miracle on the giant's leg, and the monster readily agreed. But as soon as Coyote started smashing his leg with the rock, the giant was screaming in agony. Coyote comforted him by pointing out that all the giant had to do to mend it was to spit on it. Well, the giant spat until his mouth was dry and he had nothing more to spit, but still the leg refused to mend. The pain became unbearable and finally the monster begged Coyote for help. "Just keep spitting," Coyote reassured him as he slipped out of the sweat lodge. It would be a long time before that evil giant could chase after little children again.

The Warrior Maiden
The Legend of an Oneida Heroine

Long ago, before the white man came to North America, the Oneida were constantly beset upon by their old enemies, the neighboring Mingoe. It was a terrible time: Mingoe warriors attacked the Oneida villages, set fire to their longhouses, and destroyed their cornfields. They killed all the men and boys they could find and abducted the women and girls.

The Oneida were so outnumbered that those who survived deserted their villages and fled through the forests up to the rocks and caves of the surrounding mountains. There, they were faced with a terrible dilemma: they could stay where they were and die of starvation, or they could creep down to the forest to search for food and almost certainly be caught and killed by Mingoe warriors. The tribal elders called a council out on a large cliff, well hidden from the forest below, but no one could suggest a way out—until a young girl named Aliquipiso came forward and asked to be heard.

Aliquipiso told them the Great Spirit had sent her a dream showing her how to save her people. She pointed out that the mountainside above the cliff was covered with large boulders and heavy, sharp rocks. She told them to collect as many of these as they could and then wait for her signal.

Awed by the girl's courage and wisdom, they did what she suggested. That night, Aliquipiso crept down from the cliff and into the forest by way of a secret path. As the day dawned, she wandered around the woods, pretending to be lost. It didn't take long for the Mingoe scouts to find her. They took her at once to their warrior chief who ordered the girl tied to a stake and tortured with fire until she told them where her people were hiding.

For hours, Aliquipiso refused to say a word to her tormentors. Then, at last, she pretended that the pain had become too much for her and agreed to lead them to the place where her people were hiding.

That night, hundreds of Mingoe warriors from all over the countryside gathered at the campsite. They bound Aliquipiso's hands behind her back and pushed her ahead of them to lead the way, threatening to kill her if she made one wrong move. Soundlessly, the warriors crept behind her as she led them through thickets and across streams, until they finally reached the foot of the towering cliff where the Oneida were hidden.

Nomadic and warlike, the buffalo-hunting peoples of the Plains have given the world its classic image of the traditional Native American way of life. Many Plains cultures believed in an all-powerful Great Spirit such as Wakan Tanka among the Lakota and Tirawa among the Pawnee.

"Come closer, Mingoe warriors," she whispered to them, "so you can all hear me. The Oneida are sleeping soundly right on that cliff above us, thinking they're safe. Gather around me and I'll tell you how to find the secret path that leads up to the cliff." As they crowded around Aliquipiso, she suddenly cried out, "Now, my people! They're here! Crush them!"

The Mingoe warriors had no time to flee the rocks and boulders that started raining down on them. It seemed as though the whole mountain had crumbled and buried them. So many Mingoe warriors died that night that those who survived no longer had the heart to attack and pillage the Oneida. They returned to their own hunting grounds and never again made war on Aliquipiso's people.

As for the Oneida, they told the story of the girl's incredible courage and self-sacrifice forever after, handing the legend down from grandparent to grandchild for the rest of time. It is said the Great Spirit changed Aliquipiso's beautiful spirit into two sacred plants: her hair is now the healing woodbine, and her body the fragrant honeysuckle, which is known among the Oneida as the "blood of brave women."

opposite
Like other cultures of the Northwest Pacific Coast, the Tlingit of southern Alaska (who have two Ravens—cultural hero and trickster) depicted their animal totems on everything from clothing to buildings to cooking and eating utensils.

The Hungry Hero
A Trickster Tale from the Northwest Pacific Coast

Raven stories play a popular role in many Northwest Pacific Coast cultures, especially among the Tlingit, Haida, and Tsimshian peoples. Raven is not only one of their principal cultural heroes, he's also an infamous trickster whose insatiable appetite often gets him into trouble. While it's true that tricksters everywhere tend to overeat, Raven outdoes them all, as can be seen in the following story about Raven and the fisherman.

above
Raven, the trickster hero of the Northwest, is said to be black because he was punished for bringing humans fire from the sky. This sculpture shows Raven when he was still white.

One day, just for fun, Raven stuck a red robin feather in his hair and then walked through the village. When the wife of one of the village fishermen saw him, she immediately decided she had to have a feather just like it for her own hair and asked him where she could get one. Raven remembered hearing that this woman was supposed to be the best cook in the village and his eyes lit up with mischief. He said he'd be happy to show her husband where there were lots of robin feathers.

The next day, Raven and the fisherman paddled out to a deserted, wooded island to hunt for robins. Actually, there were no robins on that island at all, but Raven tricked the fisherman into believing there were hundreds. While the fisherman was looking the other way, Raven took pieces of rotten wood and threw them up into the trees, putting a spell on them so that they changed into robins. Then Raven told the fisherman that the most beautiful robins lived on the center of the island and sent him deeper and deeper into the woods. Raven soon slipped away and raced back alone to the canoe.

Raven quickly paddled back to the mainland, where he turned himself into a large man with a face just like the fisherman's. He walked into the fisherman's cottage, where the fisherman's wife was preparing a big meal. She assumed it was her returning husband and placed his dinner on the table. Raven gulped down everything on his plate, then ate everything on hers, and then licked out the pots.

Just as he was finishing, the real fisherman returned home and was outraged to find Raven sitting at *his* table eating *his* dinner, especially since Raven had abandoned him out on that island and left him to swim home. On top of all that, when the fisherman threw down his soggy bagful of dead robins, the birds immediately changed back into a heap of rotten wood. That did it: he became so enraged that he chased Raven around the house until he caught him and clubbed him into insensibility. Then he threw the body into the ocean.

Before long, a hungry halibut came along and swallowed Raven's lifeless body whole. Once

158 Heroes of Native North American Mythology

inside the big fish, however, Raven revived and changed himself back into his old bird shape and tickled the fish until it went crazy and swam up on the shore. A number of delighted fishermen grabbed the huge fish and began to cut it up for cooking. To their astonishment, when they cut open its belly, Raven burst out and started cawing madly. "If you don't leave with your families at once," he cried, "I'll destroy you all!" The fishermen were so frightened they ran home, gathered up their wives and children, and fled to another village. What Raven counted on, of course, was that they would leave their food supplies behind. They did.

In many cultures, warriors drew on the power spirit of Thunder. Among the Iroquois, this spirit took on a human form in the personification of Hino, Guardian of the Sky. The Lakota believed the Thunderbird Wakinyan could help them battle malevolent spirits.

Glooscap Fights the Water Monster
An Algonquian Tale from the Northeast

In the myths and legends of many Algonquian cultures, Glooscap (sometimes spelled Gluskap) is the first man, a cultural hero, a trickster, and a god all rolled into one. His amazing exploits include conquering a race of magic giants and matching wits with an evil race of sorcerers. He defeated Pamola, the wicked spirit of the night and destroyed hundreds of fiends, goblins, cannibals, and witches. It seems there was no greater hero on earth than the awe-inspiring Glooscap.

Legend has it that he still lives somewhere at the southern edge of the world. He never grows old and will never die, although sometimes he gets so tired of running the world and advising people how to live that he throws up his hands and says, "That's it. I'm tired of all this and I'm going to die now." With that, he paddles off in his magic white canoe and disappears into the clouds, but people know that he'll come back. Legend says that he always comes back—he doesn't have it in his heart to abandon us forever because he knows we can't live without him.

Glooscap created everything in the world with the welfare of human beings in mind, but sometimes his original creations needed a little adjusting. When he formed the first squirrel, for example, it was as big as a whale and started chewing up whole trees like they were nothing more than little acorns. The first beaver was as big as a mountain and dammed up so much water that it flooded the country from horizon to horizon. Even moose were so huge they flattened mountains as they walked. So Glooscap went around and gave these first creatures a gentle tap on the back of the head to make them shrink to a less destructive size, which is why they are the size they are today. But some animals, like the ugly toad, were made small for other reasons, as this story explains.

When Glooscap created the first village, he taught the people there about hunting, fishing, and raising children. He made sure the village had a spring that always flowed with pure, clear, cold water—that is, until the day when it mysteriously ran dry. It even stayed dry through the spring when the snows melted and the rains came. By summer, the village elders were very worried and sent a man north to find the source of the spring and why it had run dry.

The man walked for a long time, and when he finally reached the source, he trembled in fear at what he saw. A huge, disgusting monster was sitting in a deep hole he had dug in the valley and in which he had damned up all of the spring's water. The monster was so gigantic that the top of his head disappeared in the clouds. The water around him stank with filth and poison, and the hideous monster sat in the middle of it, filling the whole valley and grinning from ear to ear, warts as big as mountains sticking out all over from his bloated body. The monster stared at the man with his dull, yellow protruding eyes and asked him what he wanted.

The man was terrified, but spoke up anyway and explained how his people were dying of thirst because the giant was hoarding all the water. In answer, the monster opened his mouth wide enough for the man to see the bits and pieces of all the many creatures he had recently killed stuck between his teeth. When he smacked his lips like a clap of thunder, the frightened man bolted and ran for home as fast as he could. He told his people in despair that there was nothing they could possibly do to get the monster to give up the water.

When Glooscap heard about all this, he knew he had to set things right and the only way to do that was to fight the monster himself. That took careful preparation. First he made himself twelve feet tall and painted his body blood red with bright yellow rings around his eyes. Then he added two huge clamshell earrings and a hundred black and white eagle feathers. For a weapon, he grabbed a nearby mountain and crushed it flat in his hand until it became a deadly flint knife with a blade as sharp as a weasel's tooth.

Now he was ready. He twisted his mouth up into his worst snarl and summoned a cloud of thunder and lightning to encircle him as he stomped off to confront the deadly giant.

"Slimy lump of mud!" he cried. "You're wallowing in water that belongs to my people—and you're turning it into slime!" With that the two started fighting and the very mountains shook as they threw each other around. The earth split open and the forests burst into flames. Just as it looked as though the monster would swallow up Glooscap with his mile-wide mouth, Glooscap made himself taller than a mountain; while the monster was trying to figure out what to do next, Glooscap took the great flint knife he had made and used it to slit the monster's belly from top to bottom. So much water gushed from the monster's terrible wound that it formed a mighty river that tumbled and foamed down the mountains, past the villages, and out toward the sea.

As for the monster, Glooscap took what was left of him and squashed him in his palm until he squeezed him into a nasty-looking little toad. Then he took the slimiest part of the water and flung it with the toad off into another valley, creating the world's first swamp. It's said that the monster's relatives still live there to this day.

This ceremonial Iroquois rattle depicts Hino the Thunder Spirit, Guardian of the Sky.

Heroes of Native North American Mythology **161**

Native American myths reinforced a strong spiritual belief in the creative force present in all living and non-living things.

The Little People

One of the most vivid recurring themes in North American Indian mythology is a conflict between opposites: good versus evil, strong versus weak, and clever versus stupid, for example. In many hero stories, the conflict is often between large and small. And it's generally not the big strong guys who are the heroes. Instead, Indian cultural heroes are often elfin in size, ranging from about ten inches (25.4cm) to three feet (3.6m) in height. They are portrayed as highly intelligent and brave, and, whether human or magical, they perform remarkable deeds to help mankind. (Giants, on the other hand, are usually portrayed as the villains—strong but oafish, evil, and more than a bit stupid.)

The twin war gods in Pueblo mythology are dwarf-size, and so is the Naskapi cultural hero Djokábesh. Like many small heroes, *Djokábesh* is a monster-slayer whose numerous exploits include killing monster bears, man-eating fish, and fierce cannibal women. It's even said he snared the sun so as to teach it not to be so hot. The legends of the Yurok Indians of northern California tell of the *woge*, a race of little people so old and wise that they remember helping to save mankind during the first flood.

Even cultures who do not have dwarf heroes (like the Wabanaki, Mohawk, and Iroquois) have magical elves and fairies who live in caves or inside rocks and trees, and have the power to grant wishes to humans who befriend them. Not all the magical little people are alike, however. Some, like the *kiwalatamos'suk*, are said to have the gift of prophecy, while the *lumpegwonos'suk* live in water and brew a magic soup that's used to make people fall in love. It's also been said that they know how to make bread out of snow.

Some little people, like the *pukalutumush* of the Micmac, are just mischievous pranksters who love to play tricks on humans at night, like hiding household items and tying knots in their horses' manes.

White Buffalo Woman
A Lakota Sioux Legend

One summer many, many years ago, the seven councils of the Lakota nation came together to light a sacred council fire to discuss their plight: there was no game and their people were starving. Each day scouts went out hunting and each day they came home empty-handed.

One day, while two of the scouts were out searching for food, a strange mist suddenly floated up on a hillside ahead of them. As they got closer, the mist lifted and they saw a beautiful young maiden with long, raven-black hair and a tanned, buffalo skin outfit so purely white that it glowed. Her clothes were embroidered with sacred designs in radiant colors they had never seen before, and her dark eyes sparkled with great power.

It would have been obvious to almost anyone that this White Buffalo Woman was a *wakan*, a holy spirit, who had to be treated with great respect. But one of the two scouts saw only a beautiful woman whom he wanted to possess and reached out in his lust to touch her. He was instantly covered by a cloud of rattlesnakes who, in a matter of minutes, reduced him to a mere pile of bones.

The other scout, however, greeted the White Buffalo Woman with the awe and respect she deserved and was therefore entrusted with a message to bring back to his camp. The woman asked the young hunter to tell his chief to prepare the camp for her arrival by building a special medicine lodge with a sacred altar. She taught him the sacred prayers and rituals that his people needed to perform.

The Lakota people followed the instructions exactly, and four days later, the White Buffalo Woman approached the camp, carrying a bundle wrapped in buffalo skin which she presented to the chief. The holy thing it contained was the *chanupa*, the sacred pipe of the Buffalo Nation. She showed the chief how to hold the pipe by its stem and bowl and explained how the smoke from its fire was Tunkashila's breath, the living breath of Great-Grandfather Mystery.

The Plains Indians, who depended on the buffalo for food, shelter, and clothing, honored the spirit of the animal in many sacred myths and rituals.

As long as the Lakota revered this pipe, she said, they would be a great nation. Then the White Buffalo Woman walked off in the same direction from which she came. Just before she disappeared over the horizon, she stopped, rolled over four times, and turned into a white buffalo calf. As soon as she vanished, great herds of buffalo appeared on the plains, allowing themselves to be killed so that the people could survive. And from that day on, the buffalo supplied the Lakota with everything they needed: meat for food, hides for clothing and shelter, and bones for tools.

above
The medicines used by Native American cultures included both medicinal herbs and sacred ritual objects, reflecting the view that an illness is always both spiritual and physical.

opposite
The giant lumberjack Paul Bunyon and his sidekick Babe the Blue Ox were just two of the folk heroes of the European settlers of the eighteenth and ninteenth centuries.

Hero Myths of the European Newcomers

The European settlers who started arriving in the mid-seventeenth century and the Africans they kidnapped and brought to North America as slaves had their folk heroes, too. Some, like Paul Bunyan, Pecos Bill, Rip van Winkle, and Brer Rabbit were purely tall tales—the inventions of storytellers—while others, like Johnny Appleseed, Mike Fink, Davey Crockett, and John Brown, were real-life heroes who were inflated into near superhumans with fabulous strength, courage, and endurance, heroes whose exploits and adventures often became exaggerated, romanticized legends.

One of the best-known heroes of the tall-tale variety is Paul Bunyan. It's said that Paul Bunyan was a gigantic lumberjack of such superhuman strength that just by swinging his great ax in a circle around him, he could chop down every tree within a one-mile (1.6km) radius. It took twelve boys with bacon fastened to their feet to grease his pancake griddle each morning. His constant companion and helper, Babe the Blue Ox, was so huge he could drink rivers dry and his shoes were so heavy that a blacksmith carrying just one sank knee-deep into solid rock at every step.

Pecos Bill, another purely mythological hero, was supposedly a legendary cowboy who was raised by coyotes and whose exploits include scooping out the Grand Canyon and putting fishhooks into his liquor to give it more kick. Rip van Winkle was a New England character who

164 Heroes of Native North American Mythology

got so drunk playing ninepins with a bunch of ghostly Catskill Dutchmen that he passed out and slept for twenty years while the world changed around him. Brer Rabbit was the trickster hero of a whole series of African-American animal fables told by the beloved mythical storyteller, Uncle Remus.

As for real-life mythological heroes, there really was an American pioneer who planted apple trees throughout Pennsylvania, Ohio, and Indiana, but Johnny Appleseed (as John Chapman came to be known) quickly became a larger-than-life character who was said to roam the countryside carrying his seed sack in one hand and his Bible in the other, wearing a coffee sack for a shirt and saucepan for a hat. In some stories, he not only spent his life flinging appleseeds throughout the countryside, his very steps forever changed the American landscape.

Mike Fink was a real fur trader and boatman along the Mississippi River who was forever getting himself in and out of dangerous adventures. The stories of his exploits and abilities were often greatly exaggerated, if not outright fictionalized. He was such a crack shot, supposedly, that he could drive a nail into wood with a bullet from a hundred yards (91.4m) away.

Another crack shot (and legendary figure) was Davey Crockett, ace frontier scout and Indian fighter, who became the romanticized hero of countless books, movies, and even a television series. John Brown was a true hero, a radical abolitionist and expert guerrilla fighter whose fierce fights against pro-slavery forces in the years before the Civil War helped make him a larger-than-life legend. After he was hanged in 1859 for his most famous exploits (the seizing of a government arsenal at Harper's Ferry) he became a hero and martyr to blacks and Northerners with anti-slavery sentiments. The true stories of John Brown's heroic deeds often became romanticized and exaggerated in the many stories and songs that were later written about him.

Weak from fasting, Wunzh suddenly saw an appariton descend from the sky and challenge him to a wrestling match.

Wunzh and the Origin of Maize
An Ojibwa Hero Myth

Many historians believe the following story inspired parts of Longfellow's poem "Hiawatha."

A long time ago there was a poor man who lived with his wife and children in a very beautiful part of the country. This man was not just poor, however; he had so little knowledge about how to find food for his family that they often went hungry. But he was a kind man, nevertheless, and a person who always gave thanks to the Great Spirit for everything he and his family did receive. He taught his children to do the same.

The man's oldest son was named Wunzh, and when the boy turned fifteen, he became old enough to undertake the *Keiguishimowin*, the ritual fast which would determine what kind of spirit would be his guardian and spiritual guide throughout his life. His father built him a small lodge in a secluded spot, where he could be alone to meditate.

Wunzh spent the first two days rambling through the woods, wondering about all the plant life. He realized that there must be many plants his family could eat, but how could one tell which were good to eat and which were poi-

sonous? He realized that if a person could understand how plants grew, they could grow them instead of having to depend on foraging through the forests looking for them. During those first two days, he came to hope that his vision, when it arrived, would not be one that made him a great warrior or a healer or a hunter, but instead would show him an easier way than hunting and fishing to get food for his family.

By his third day of fasting, Wunzh felt so weak and faint that he stayed in the bed of leaves he had made for himself on the forest floor. Suddenly he saw an apparition coming toward him from the sky, a handsome youth dressed all in yellow with a magnificent plume of green feathers on his head. "I am sent by the Great Spirit to teach you how to help your people," the apparition said. "But even though you do not seek fame as a warrior, you must pass certain tests."

With that, the apparition challenged Wunzh to a wrestling match. Weak as the boy was, he did his best and they wrestled for a long time until he could hold out no longer. The next day the spirit returned and challenged Wunzh to another wrestling match, and although the boy was even weaker than he had been the day before, he courageously accepted the challenge and wrestled again until he was exhausted. The day after that was the same, except that when they finished, the spirit took Wunzh into the small lodge and told him that there was just one more test to pass before he could be rewarded with what he desired. This was to be the hardest test of all.

"Tomorrow," he told Wunzh, "we will wrestle one last time. This time you will win the match and kill me. When I am dead, you are to clean the roots and weeds off a sunny plot of earth, bury me there, and then leave. But you

with food to bring him back from his vision quest. In the months that followed, he asked his son many times if he had had a vision, but Wunzh refused to tell a soul about what had happened to him. When he returned to tend the secluded grave, he always did so in secret, and even though he did not know what it was supposed to mean, he never lost faith.

One day when he got to the spot, he was amazed to see the green plumes of the spirit's headpiece coming up through the ground, and in the weeks that followed he watched with great delight as they grew into a tall, graceful plant with brightly colored silken hair and golden clusters on each side.

Finally understanding the great vision he had been given, Wunzh brought his father to see the magnificent plant, which he introduced as his dear friend Mondawmin (maize). Wunzh learned from his spirit friend how to pull the husks from the golden cobs, and how to grind, cook, and bake the kernels of maize. He learned how to plant some of the kernels and how to tend the growing plants until they brought forth corncobs of their own.

must keep coming back to keep the grass and weeds from my grave and to see if I have returned to life. Under no circumstances are you to tell anyone, even your father, about this."

When the spirit returned the next day, Wunzh did everything he had been instructed to do. The next day, Wunzh's father showed up

That was how Wunzh's people received the gift of corn. Each year they held a special feast in honor of the Great Spirit who had shown them that they no longer had to rely on hunting for food. They gave special thanks to the Great Spirit for sending this vision to Wunzh.

Historians believe Longfellow based his poem Hiawatha *on the Ojibwa warrior hero Wunzh.*

Heroes of Native North American Mythology

Conclusion

Study the myths and legends of any culture in the world—past and present—and you'll find that the one common theme they all share are heroes who perform extraordinary feats of bravery and risk the hazards of fantastic journeys to benefit mankind.

As we've seen in the stories presented in this book, in most mythologies, ordinary humans are powerless against gods who see and use them as their playthings, as chess pieces to be moved, played and sacrificed as they see fit. Heroes defy the gods on behalf of mankind. They refuse to give in no matter what obstacles the gods put in their way. No matter how difficult, they perform all the tasks the gods put before them, and whether by bravery, trickery, endurance, or a simple refusal to submit to their fate, heroes impress the gods so much that the gods allow them to continue living. In some cultures, the hero even becomes a god or demigod himself.

These great heroes, whether in human shape or transformed into animals, meet fantastic people and creatures along their journey, often performing what are seen as great miracles or feats of power on the way to fulfill their quest. It's no wonder their adventures are told and retold for centuries, often long after the cultures themselves have grown and changed.

A noted scholar and popular mythologist named Joseph Campbell spent a lifetime studying and comparing the hero myths of different cultures. In his book, The Hero With a Thousand Faces, he states, "A legendary hero is usually the founder of something—the founder of a new age, the founder of a new religion, the founder of a new city, the founder of a new way of life. In order to found something new, one has to leave the old and go in quest of the seed idea, a germinal idea that will have the potentiality of bringing forth that new thing."

Looking at the story of the hero's quest in mythologies from around the world, Campbell found great similarities. Look back at the hero stories in this book and you'll see that they follow a three-stage pattern: the hero's Departure, his Journey and his Return.

The hero departs from the everyday world of common people into a region of supernatural wonder, a world that is unfamiliar and strange to him. There is always a call to adventure in some form, some signal which calls the hero forth upon his journey, although the hero may not recognize the call or may even initially refuse it.

When he does finally accept the call, the hero ventures forward and passes through a gate that divides the world he has known into the world of his quest. Now his adventures have really begun. This journey is often represented in mythology as being upon a path over land, a voyage upon water, or a frightening descent into the Underworld. On this journey, the hero must often complete tasks, such as the feats of Hercules, or overcome great obstacles and fight monsters, as Glooskap did. The journey can also be in quest of a reunion with a beloved or of an object that can be brought back to heal or better society, such as the use of fire.

Some heroes like Coyote and Great Spider change shape on their adventures. Some have humorous exploits, like Maui or Qat when they use cunning to outwit the gods.

Although the journey is always a very personal one for the hero, his achievements must always be shared with his community wen he

returns, as Maui did in Polynesia when he brought islands to the surface from the bottom of the sea and captured and harnessed the Sun. This stage is sometimes the hardest, however, because the hero's hard-won wisdom and achievements are often rejected by the very people they are meant to benefit.

Hero myths appeal to us on several different levels. First of all, they are often terrific adventure stories, filled with harrowing escapes, bloody battles, and buried treasure, in which the forces of good always triumph over evil. Second, on a deeper level, the hero's journey reflects our passage each of us has to experience to transcend to a higher spiritual level. And third, the hero's journey represents our collective growth as a community as well as the spiritual growth of mankind.

Whether personal or cosmic, the journey is always upon a razor's edge, that sharp and narrow line upon which a hero must walk in the quest for self-discovery. The more you read of the thousands of exotic hero legends from all the corners of the world and from all eras of history, the more you will understand how much alike we really are.

Perseus, like all great heroes, risked a fate worse than death when he set off to slash off the head of the hideous gorgon Medusa.

Conclusion **171**

INDEX

A

Aborigines, 103, 106, *106*
Achilles, 29
Acrisius, (King of Argos), 30, 34
Aegeus (King), 34, 35, 36
Aethra, 34
Africa, 9, *9*, 118–133
Aillen, 51
Aiwel Longar, 130–131
Ajax, 29
Akokoa, 125–126
Aladdin, 8, 24–27
Alcavilu, 147–150
"Ali Baba and the Forty Thieves," 20, 21
Aliquipiso, 156–157
Amaterasu, 101
Amazons, 39
Anansi, 120–122
Andromeda, 30, *31*, 33, 34
Andvari, 75, 76, 79, 81
Anglo-Saxons, 45, 64
Annallja Tu Bari, 126, 128–129
Aonbharr, 52, 53
Aphrodite, 42, 43
Arabia, 18
Arabian Nights, 9
Argonauts, 40, 41
Argos, 30, 34, 37
Ariadne, 35, 36
Artemis, 40
Arthur, King, 8, 45, 59, *59*, 60–61, *60–61*
Asia, 84–101
Atalanta, 40, 41, *41*, 42, *42–43*, 43
Athena, 29, 32, 39
Atlas, 32–33, 39
Atli, 80, 82
Augean stables, 37
Australia, 102–117

B

Balder, 70
Beowulf, 8, 9, 45, 64–65
Bikramajit, 91
Blue Falcon, 54, 55, 57
The Book of Ballymote, 46
The Book of Leinster, 46
The Book of the Dean of Lismore, 46
The Book of the Dun Cow, 46
Borghild, 74, 75
Botoque, 151
Bran, 51, 52
Branstock, 68, 69
Brer Rabbit, 119, 164, 166
Britain, 44–65
Brünnhilde, 83
Brynhild, 8, 78, 81
Bull of Heaven, 17

C

Cailleach Bheare, 53
Calydonian boar, 41
Camelot, 59
Cannibalism, 12, 15
Cap of Darkness, 32
Celts, 45, 53, 61
Centaurs, 36
Cepheus, (King of Phoenicia), 33
Cerberus, 37, *37*
Cerynita, 37
Chaos, 101
Ch'ih Pi, 92–94
China, 92–96
Chiron, 36
Chumong, 88
Cleomedes of Astypalia, 8
Comari, 23
Conan, 52
Conn Ceadchathach, 51
Coyote, 154–156
Creon (King of Thebes), 37
Cretan bull, 39
Crete, 35
Cuchulain, 53
Cults, 11

D

Daedalus, 35
DalnAraidhe, 51
Danaë, 30
Debauchery, 9, 15, 17
Deianeira, *38*, 39
Delphic oracle, 37
Demons, 11, 96, *96*
Deucalion (King), 92
Dinarzade, 18, 20, 21
Diomedian horses, 39
Dionysus, 36
Dragons, 34, 53, 85, 86, 88
Dreamtime, 103, 106, 107
Dwarves, 21, 70, 75, 83, 96, 138

E

Eddas, 67, 77, *77*
Egypt, 10–15
El Dorado, 146
Elves, 50, 70
Elylimil, 75
Enkidu, 16, 17
Epic of Gilgamesh, 9
Erythia, 39
Erytion, 41
Eurytheus (King of Argos), 37, 39
Excalibur, 59

F

Fafnir, 69, 75, 76, 78, *78*
Fates, 29
Fianna of Erin, 46, 51, 52
Finn MacCool, 46, 49, 51, 52, 53
Floods, 17, 92, 107–108
Folklore, 45
Fomoire, 52
Fomorians, 46
Frazer, James, 7
Freud, Sigmund, 7
Frey, 70, 73, *73*
Freyja, 70
Frigg, 68
Funeral
    games, 42
    pyres, 81, 83, 138
    sarcophagi, 14, *14*
    texts, 11

G

Gaki, 97
Galahad, 61
Gawain, 60
Genies, 26, 27
Geryon, 39
Giants, 34, 53, 54, 55, 70, 83
Gilgamesh, 8, 11, 15, 16, *16*, 17
Gille-Decair, 52
Gillie Martin, the Fox, 54, 55, 57
Glooscap, 160–161
Gorgons, 32
Gourd Children, 92
Grani, 78, 79
Greece, 8, 28–43
Gudrun, 79, 81, 82, *82*
Guinevere, 59, 60
Gunnar, 79, 80, 81
Gurrorm, 79, 81
Gwawl, 56, 57, 58

H

Hades, 39
Haemosu, 86–88
Hagen, 83, *83*
Hamud, 74
Heimdal, 70
Helgi Hundingsbane, 74
Henge, 96, 97, *97*
Hera, 29, 36, 37, 39
Heracles, 6, 7, 8, 9, 29, 34, 36, 37, *37*, 38, 39
Hermes, 29, 32
Heroes
    ancestor, 110
    celestial, 86
    cultural, 8
    princes, 18
    traditional, 8–9
    trickster, 9, 70, 103, 109, 110, 117, 158
    warrior, 8
Hesperides, 39
Hina, 110
Hïnir, 75
Hippolyta, 39
Hjordis, 75
Hogni, 81
Holy Grail, 60
Horus, 12, *13*, 15
Hunding, 78
Huwawa, 17
Hydra, 6, 7

I

Iain, Prince, 54
Iliad, 9
India, 89–91
Infidelity, 18, 36
Ireland, 45, 46–53
Ishtar, 17
Isis, 12, *13*, 14–15
Ittan-momen, 97
Izanagi and Izanami, 100–101

J

Jason, 41
Jigoku, 96, 97
Johnny Appleseed, 164
Jung, Carl, 7

K

Kae, 110, 112
Kappa, 96
Karan (King), 89–91
Knights of the Round Table, 45, 59, *59*, 60–61, *60–61*
Korea, 86–88
Kukailmoku, 112, *112*
Kukunoshi, 100
Kûmwa (King), 87, 88
Kwasi Benefo, 131–133

L

Labyrinth, 34, 35
Lady of the Lake, 59, 60
Lancelot, 60, 61
Larissa, 34
Legends, 8, 45, 67
Leprechauns, 50, *50*

Lernian Hydra, 37
Liki, 75
Ljod, 68
Loki, 70, 76, 83
Luaghaidh Lagha, 51
Lugh, 52
Lyngvi, 75

M

Mabinogion, 57, 60
Magic, 24, 27, 54, 79, 101, 155
    fans, 96
    helmet, 100
    leaves, 147
    peaches, 101
    runes, 75, 78
    swords, 73
    wine, 98
Mag Moullach, 53
Mahuika, 104
Manu, 92
Marawa, 112–113
Maui, 104–106
Medea, 34
Medusa, 30, 32, 33, *33*
Megara, 37
Melanion, 42, *42–43*, 43
Meleager, 40, 41
Merlin the Magician, 59, 60, 61
Middle East, 10–11
Minamoto-no-Yorimitsu, 97–100
Minos (King of Crete), 34, 35
Minotaur, 34, 35, *35*
Mjollnir, 70
Mmoboro, 120
The Monkey King, 95–96
Monsters, 33, 53, 55, 96, 103
Mordred, 59, 60

Mount Erymanthus, 37
Muses, 29
Mycenae, 37, 39
Myths
    African, 118–133
    ancestor, 85
    Asian, 84–101
    Australian, 102–117
    British, 44–65
    Chinese, 92–96
    creation, 53, 101, 119
    Egyptian, 10–15
    fertility, 125
    flood, 17, 92, 107–108
    god, 140
    Greek, 28–43
    Indian, 89–91
    Irish, 46–53
    Japanese, 96–101
    Korean, 86–88
    Latin American, 134–151
    Native American, 152–169
    Oceanic, 102–117
    Scandinavian, 66–83
    Scottish, 45, 53–57
    traditional, 131
    Welsh, 45, 57–61

N

Native Americans, 9, 152–169
Naxos, 36
Nereids, 33
Nibelungen, 67, 83, *83*
Nimean lion, 37
North America, 9, 152–169
Nurikabe, 97
Nymphs, 32

O

Oceania, 9, 102–117
Odin, 68, 69, 75
Oedipus, 7
Oeneus (King of Calydon), 40
Ogbe Baba Akinyelure, 124–125
Ogres, 21, 96
Ohowatatsumi, 100
Old Man Coyote, 9
Old Man of the Sea, 23
Olifat, 114–117
Olympics, 9
Oni, 96, 98
Onini, 120, 122
Onyame, 120, 122
Osebo, 120, 122
Osiris, 12, *13*, 14, 15, *15*
Oter, 75
Otherworld, 50, 51, 52, 54, 61

P

Pangu, 101
Paul Bunyan, 164, *165*
Pele, 109, *109*
Peleus, 41, 42
Perseus, 8, 8, 30, *31*, 32–34
Persia, 23
Pharaohs, 12, 14
Phoenicia, 14
Polydectes, 30
Polynesia, 103
Popol Vuh, 9, 140
Poseidon, 29, 33
Priests, 11, 131, 140, 146
Prometheus, 8
Pwyll, 56, 57, 58, 58

Q

Qat, 112–113
Quetzalcoatl, 136–140

R

Ra, 12
Ragnarok, 70
Raven, 9, 158–160
Regin, 76, 78
Reidmar, 76
Rerir, 68
Rhiannon, 57, 58, 58
River Earl, 86–88
Robin Hood, 62, 63
Runes, 75, 78, 79, 79

S

Salmon of Knowledge, 49, 51
Samba Gana, 126, 128–129
Sasabonsam, 125–126
Scandinavia, 66–83
Sceolaing, 51
Schahriar, 18, 18, 20, 21
Scheherazade, 18, 18, 20, 21
Scorpion Man, 11
Scotland, 45, 53–57
Seriphus, 30, 32, 34
Serpents, 17, 32, 76, 78, 103, 108, 128
Set, 12, 14, 15
Shape-shifters, 9
Shimatsuhiko, 100
Shinbenkidokushu, 98, 99
Shuten Doji, 97, 99, 100
Siegfried, 76, 78, 83
Siggeir, 68, 69, 73
Sigi, 68
Sigmund, 8, 68, 69, 73, 74, 75
Signy, 68, 69, 73
Sigridrifa, 78
Sigrun, 74
Sigurd, 69, 75, 78, 81, *81*
Sinbad the Sailor, 21, *21*, 22, 23, *23*
Sinfjotli, 73, 74, 75
Skalds, 67
Slave of the Ring, 25
Sleipnir, 68, *68*, 70
Sorcerers, 34, 69
South America, 9
Spider Woman, 9
Stymphalian birds, 39
Sumeria, 11

T

Taboos, 9
Takehayasusanowo, 101
Tengu, 96
Tezcatlipoca, 137, 138
Thebes, 37
Theseus, 8, 34, 35, *35*, 36, *36*
Thor, 70, *71*
Thousand and One Nights, 18–27
Titans, 32
Tongmyûng (King), 88
Troezen, 34
Tuna the Eel, 104, 109
Tunua-nui, 110
Twelve Books of Poetry, 46
Twins, 129, 132, 140–144

U

Uime, 51
Uncle Remus, 119, 166
Underworld, 15, 37, 39, 85
Uruk, 15, 16, 17

V

Valhalla, 68, 70, 83
Valkyries, 68, 78, 79, 83
Volsung, 67, 68–82, 83

W

Wales, 45, 57–61
Waters of Death, 17
Wawalak Sisters, 103, 107–108
Wen Zhong, 92
White Buffalo Woman, 163
Wildflower, 86–88
William the Conqueror, 45
Wotan, 70, 83
Wunzh, 166, *167*, 168–169

Y

The Yellow Book of Lecan, 46
Yellow Filly, 55, 57
Yin and Yang, 93, 101
Yorimitsu, 98
Yurlunggur, 106, 107, 108
Yü the Great, 92

Z

Zeus, 8, 29, 30, 32, 36, 92

PHOTOGRAPHY CREDITS

AKG Photos: pp. 69, 76, 77, 78, 79, 80, 81, 82, 83, 142, 144, 151

American Museum of Natural History/Courtesy Department Library Services: Neg# 328740: p. 159

Art Resource, NY: pp. 15, 59, 90, 97; Bridgeman: pp. 8, 19, 22, 26, 98-99; Giraudon: pp. 13, 16, 36, 47, 89, 94, 171; Erich Lessing: pp. 2, 31, 32-33, 35, 37, 38, 53, 54, 93; Nimatallah: p. 14; The Pierpont Morgan Library: p. 60-61; Scala: p. 6, 25, 42-43; SEF: pp. 41, 88, 105; Aldo Tutino: p. 132; Werner Forman Archive: pp. 70, 72, 73, 74, 95, 96, 109, 110, 112, 120, 138, 158, 163

©Deborah Bernhardt: pp. 49, 52

©Richard Todd Photography: pp. 121 (The Dumonstein Collection), 122 (The Baker Collection), 124 (The Walt Disney-Tishman Collection of African Art), 125, 129, 133 (Stanoff Collection)

E.T. Archive: pp. 71, 75, 100, 136, 137, 139, 140, 141, 145, 146, 148

FPG International: ©Gerald French: p. 162; ©Richard Harrington: p. 128; ©Spencer Jones: p. 164; ©Alan Kearney: p. 147; ©Robert Pastner: p. 126

©Lois Ellen Frank: p. 154

©Jason Laure: pp. 9, 123

Leo de Wys, Inc.: ©J. Aigner: p. 149; ©Leo de Wys/Sipa/Garrigues: p. 127; ©J. Dressel: p. 107; ©Richard Saunders: p. 130

North Wind Picture Archive: pp. 18, 20, 21, 23, 46, 51, 62, 63, 64, 86, 87, 108, 111, 113, 131, 150, 155, 157, 160, 161, 162, 167, 168

Sienna Art Works/©Michael Friedman Publishing Group: pp. 55, 56, 58

Superstock: pp. 48, 106, 114-115, 117; Christie's Images: p. 50

BIBLIOGRAPHY

Alpers, Anthony. *Legends of the South Seas*. New York: Thomas Y. Crowell Company, 1970.

———. *Maori Myths & Tribal Legends*. Boston: Houghton Mifflin, 1966.

Barlow, Genevieve. *Latin American Tales: From the Pampas to the Pyramids of Mexico*. Chicago: Rand McNally & Company, 1966.

Berry, Jack, transl. *West African Folktales*. Evanston, IL: Nothwestern University Press, 1991.

Bierhorst, John. *The Mythology of Mexico and Central America*. New York: William Morrow & Company, 1990.

———. *The Mythology of North America*. New York: William Morrow and Company, 1985.

Birrell, Anne. *Chinese Mythology: An Introduction*. Baltimore: The Johns Hopkins University Press, 1993.

Bullfinch, Thomas. *Bullfinch's Mythology*. Modern Library, 1993.

Burland, Cottie. *North American Indian Mythology*. New York: Tudor Publishing, 1965.

Campbell, Joseph. *Historical Atlas of World Mythology*. Vol. II. New York: Harper & Row, 1989.

Courlander, Harold. *A Treasury of African Folklore*. New York: Crown Publishers, 1975.

Davidson, Hilda. *Gods and Myths of Northern Europe*. Baltimore: Penguin Books, 1964.

Erdoes, Richard, ed. *American Indian Myths and Legends*. New York: Pantheon Books, 1984.

Goodrich, Norma Lorre. *Myths of the Hero*. New York: Orion Press, 1962.

Gray, John. *Library of the World's Myths and Legends: Near Easten Mythology*. New York: Peter Bedrick Books, 1969.

Grimal, Pierre, ed. *Larousse World Mythology*. London: Paul Hamlyn Press, 1965.

Hackin, J., and Clement Huart, et. al. *Asiatic Mythology*. New York: Thomas Y. Crowell Publishers, 1963.

Hinnels, John R. *Library of the World's Myths and Legends: Persian Mythology*. New York: Peter Bedrick Books, 1985.

Horowitz, Anthony. *Myths and Legends*. New York: Kingfisher Books, 1994.

Ions, Veronica. *Indian Mythology*. London: Paul Hamlyn Press, 1967.

Leeming, David Adams. *Mythology: The Voyage of the Hero*. New York: Harper & Row Publishers, 1981.

Munch, P.A. *Norse Mythology: Legends of the Gods and Heroes*. Translated by Sigurd Bernhard Hustvedt. New York: AMS Press, 1970.

Nicholson, Irene. *Mexican and Central American Mythology*. London: Paul Hamlyn Publishers, 1967.

Osbourne, Harold. *South American Mythology*. London: Paul Hamlyn Publishers, 1968.

Parrinder, Geoffrey. *African Mythology*. London: Paul Hamlyn Publishers, 1967.

Patrick, Richard. *All Color Book of Egyptian Mythology*. New York: Crescent Books, 1972.

Poignant, Roslyn. *Oceanic Mythology, The Myths of Polynesia, Micronesia, Melanesia, Australia*. London: Paul Hamlyn Publishers, 1967.

Reed, A.W. *Maori Legends*. David & Charles Publishers, Ltd., 1972.

Roughsey, Dick. *The Rainbow Serpent*. Milwaukee: Gareth Stevens Publishing, 1988.

Rugoff, Milton, ed. *A Harvest of World Folk Tales*. New York, The Viking Press, 1969.

Smyth, Daragh. *A Guide to Irish Mythology*. Dublin, Ireland: Irish Academic Press, 1988.

Willis, Roy ed. *World Mythology*. New York: Henry Holt & Company, 1993.

Yolen, Jane, ed. *Favorite Folktales from Around the World*. New York: Pantheon Books, 1986.